THE SUEZ WAR

THE
SUEZ WAR

PAUL JOHNSON
ASSISTANT EDITOR 'THE NEW
STATESMAN AND NATION'

Foreword by
ANEURIN BEVAN

1957
MACGIBBON & KEE
LONDON

FIRST PUBLISHED 1957
ALL RIGHTS RESERVED
MACGIBBON & KEE

PRINTED IN GREAT BRITAIN BY
THE GARDEN CITY PRESS LIMITED
LETCHWORTH, HERTFORDSHIRE

THIS BOOK IS
DEDICATED TO
MARIGOLD

CONTENTS

INTRODUCTION

THERE IS ALMOST universal bewilderment, anger and dismay about the Anglo-French adventure in Egypt. It is incomprehensible how statesmen of such experience as Sir Anthony Eden and M. Guy Mollet in particular could have brought themselves to commit such an act of folly, because even if the adventure had been successful in achieving its immediate military objectives, nevertheless it still would have been folly. If the expeditionary force had seized Port Said, Ismailia and Suez, it is still not possible to see what advantage would have been gained by France and Britain from the resulting situation. Even if Nasser himself had been brought down and a puppet régime, obedient to Britain and France's requirements, established in his place, how could such a set-up have permanently guaranteed uninterrupted passage through more than a hundred miles of canal surrounded by hostile Egyptians? Opportunities for sabotaging that thin slip of water would be innumerable. The establishment of military guards to prevent this happening, in addition to keeping order throughout Egypt, would have imposed an intolerable strain on the resources of Britain and France.

And what about the oil itself? Did the French and British Cabinets believe for one moment that the Arab nations would not feel mortally offended by a successful military *coup d'état* against one of their leading neighbours, headed by a man who stood in the eyes of the Arab world as a champion against Western Imperialism?

Could there possibly have been any assurance that the
oil would flow uninterruptedly in these circumstances?
Even granting that it is to the commercial and economic
advantage of the Arab Oil States to sell the oil to the
West, there would still remain scores of thousands of
enraged Muslims who would blow up the unguarded
pipelines stretching across the deserts.

What then was in the minds of the French and
British governments? What was the mood that led them
to seize upon means which could not possibly have
enabled them to accomplish the objectives they set
themselves? How did it come about that they abandoned
the arts of diplomacy and of negotiation and resorted
to an act which enraged their allies, offended their
friends, and dishonoured their repeatedly stated obligations to the United Nations?

I believe the explanation is to be found in a mood
of mounting frustration, for which the United States
must itself bear some share of responsibility. The
beginnings of a positive peace policy, which some of us
had come to hope for, were wrecked by the withdrawal
by the United States, followed by Britain, of finances for
the Aswan Dam in Egypt. It had long been obvious to
students of the Middle Eastern situation that the
dependence of Europe upon Middle Eastern oil required
long-term plans for the improvement of the conditions
of the masses in the Middle East; not only in the Oil
States themselves, but in the Arab countries possessing
no oil. It was foolish beyond all belief to imagine that
the populations of the Middle East would continue
docilely to see wealth flowing from their lands to sustain
the higher standards of living of Western Europe and
to create oil millionaires in Europe and in the United
States, without at the same time demanding their share.

When superimposed on this you keep in mind the
inflamed relations between Israel and her Arab neigh-

bours, stoked continuously by the existence of three-quarters of a million of refugees from Israel living in appalling squalor and poverty, then you have a state of affairs so obviously boiling up to eruption that it is difficult to forgive the governments of the United States, Britain and France for not having taken concerted action.

No doubt considerable blame attaches to Nasser for his folly in trying to play off the Western nations against Russia and vice versa, but in the absence of effective co-operation between France, Britain and the United States he could scarcely be blamed for following their example and trying to fish in the same troubled waters.

The mood of frustration, to which I have already referred, was accompanied among the followers of M. Guy Mollet and Sir Anthony Eden by a pervasive sense of nostalgia, of nostalgia for a past when the will of both countries was imposed by armed force. When you remember that Britain and France had undertaken, largely because of exhortations from across the Atlantic, a huge burden of armaments, it was difficult for the statesmen of Britain and France to conclude that these were quite useless in persuading President Nasser to yield to their wishes.

What is the purpose of a war machine of such a monstrous size if it cannot be exerted against a small, weak and recalcitrant nation? This is also the reasoning of the Soviet rulers when faced with resistance in Hungary. It is hard for people caught in the mould of conventional thinking to re-think the functions of armed force in the modern community. It is hard for them to reach the conclusion that the objectives which from time immemorial armed might has pursued, are no longer attainable by it. And that these huge war machines, intolerably burdensome in every respect, are no longer relevant to existing society. It is not merely that the heroism of the civilian, as displayed in Hungary,

makes nonsense of the power of tanks; it is also that
the war machine, whilst it can capture and hold a
specific physical military objective, is incapable of re-
shaping a whole community. It cannot be used for the
imposition of long-term social and political policies, for
these ferment and fructify in the minds of men and
women, and cannot be created and maintained by the
crude mechanisms of armies, navies and air forces.

Permanent social objectives are beyond the reach of
armed force, and yet it is to the attainment of just such
objectives that the war machines of the whole world,
including Russia and the United States, have set
themselves.

When, in addition, we reflect upon the existence of the
hydrogen bomb, it is surely obvious that a crisis has been
reached in the affairs of man where the old aptitudes
and attitudes, ancient modes of thought and conventional values, are all in the melting-pot. We either adjust
our thinking to this new state or we fumble on and
stumble on to final catastrophe.

If the monumental folly of France and of Britain will
have served the purpose of compelling us to think down
to the roots of the human dilemma, then some advantage
will be snatched from the crisis. In this little book, Mr
Paul Johnson tells the story and gives the background of
the Anglo-French action. He brings to it an intimate
experience of French politics, a wide knowledge of
international affairs, an acute mind and a brilliant pen.

Whilst I do not necessarily share every evaluation Mr
Johnson has made of the facts, nevertheless I commend
his book to all who wish to understand this tragic story.

ANEURIN BEVAN

Chapter One

PRELUDE TO CATASTROPHE

ON THE AFTERNOON of Thursday July 19 1956, Mr John Foster Dulles, the American Secretary of State, asked the Egyptian Ambassador in Washington, Mr Ahmed Hussein, to come to his office in the State Department. When the Ambassador arrived, Mr Dulles handed him a letter, in which the United States Government announced the withdrawal of its offer to contribute $56 million towards the financing of the Egyptian High Dam at Aswan. Pale with anger, Mr Hussein hurried back to his embassy to telephone the news to his Foreign Minister, Dr Fawzi, in Cairo. He was too late; Fawzi already knew. Contrary to diplomatic practice, Mr Dulles had communicated the statement to the Press before delivering it to the country concerned.

The next morning, Sir Harold Caccia, Acting Permanent Under-Secretary at the Foreign Office, informed Mr Abdul Fetouh, the Egyptian Ambassador in London, that Britain too was withdrawing its loan—a matter of $15 million. The same evening, Mr Eugene Black, President of the World Bank, announced that, owing to the Anglo-American action, the World Bank was no longer in a position to advance the $200 million which it had promised Egypt the week before.

In his letter, Mr Dulles said the reasons for America's

withdrawal were Egypt's failure to agree to various
amendments to the plan for the dam, and doubts as to
her ability to provide the sum of $700 million, which
was to be her eventual share of its cost. On the first
point, the letter was misleading : the American conditions had been stated in an *aide-mémoire* sent to Egypt
in December; most of these had been accepted by Egypt
in January, and only a week before the U.S. withdrawal
the Egyptian Ambassador had returned to Washington
from Cairo with instructions to accept the remaining
ones.

On the second point, the letter was nearer to the
mark. In the past ten months, Egypt had been buying
ever-increasing shipments of arms from behind the Iron
Curtain. In April, it was learned that she had mort-
gaged $200 million of cotton—as yet unplanted—in
exchange for Czech-produced MIG 15s and 17s, and
Stalin heavy tanks. On July 9, publication of the
Egyptian budget revealed that military expenditure was
to rise from 18 to 25 per cent of total appropriations.
During 1957, it showed, Egypt would spend £E54
million on arms and only £E2.9 million on the dam.
Egypt, it was clear to the State Department economic
experts, must inevitably fall behind on its payments
towards the project. But this fact, strangely enough,
had not caused misgivings in the World Bank. On the
contrary, on July 12 the Bank had come to a provisional
agreement with Mr Hussein, which was awaiting signa-
ture when Mr Dulles made his announcement.

What, then, were the real reasons for America's
withdrawal? There were two. First, Mr Dulles was
under severe pressure from Congress to cut foreign aid
appropriations. The Senate, anxious to finish the business

for the session and escape from the syrupy heat of Washington, was in an ugly mood. The week before, its Appropriations Committee had asked Dulles to abandon the Aswan project. He had refused—hesitantly. Then, on July 17, representatives of the Senate cotton lobby, which naturally wished to prevent the increase in Egyptian cotton production which the dam project would eventually facilitate, called on him and extracted from him the promise that he would reconsider the matter.

The fact was, Dulles was moving—in his usual haphazard and unsystematic manner—towards a major policy decision. Ever since the war, America had supported Egypt, both as a counter to British colonialism in the Middle East and as a proof of its friendship for the up-and-coming nations of Asia and Africa. The U.S. Ambassador in Cairo, Charles Byroade, was a fervent Egyptophile and well disposed to the Nasser régime. He was moreover, fully backed up by his chief in the State Department, Mr George Allen, in charge of the Middle Eastern desk. Allen, who disliked colonialism, was instrumental in preventing America from joining the British-sponsored Baghdad Pact, and in forging firm bonds of friendship with Saudi Arabia, Britain's traditional enemy on the Persian Gulf. Together, these two men had succeeded in making support for Nasser the linchpin of America's Middle Eastern policy.

But for some months before that fatal Thursday afternoon, Dulles had been eyeing Nasser with increasing dislike. Nasser's decision, in September 1955, to buy Communist arms had allowed Russia, in one move, to leap

over Britain's ramshackle 'Northern Tier' and to
become, for the first time in her history, an effective
Middle Eastern Power. Dulles disliked seeing MIG 15s
unloading in Alexandria. He disliked even more hearing
that the Russian Embassy in Cairo had increased its
staff from forty to 150, and that Russian technicians
were pouring into Egypt. He disliked also being prodded
and nagged at by the British for backing Nasser. He
disliked too the increasing improvidence and rapacity
of Nasser's Saudi Arabian allies, who were already two
years overdrawn on their oil revenues, and who had, in
May, suddenly decided to increase the rent payable for
the American atomic bomber base at Daihran. Dulles
had been brooding on these grievances for some time.
But what finally made him change his mind was the
news that Nasser was to take part in a meeting on the
Yugoslav island of Brioni with Nehru and Tito. It was,
the Press announced, a 'conference of the neutralist
Powers', and it was taking place without Dulles' consent
or encouragement. He read the papers, crowded with
photographs of the Brioni junketings, with increasing
irritation. Within a few days, he had come to a decision,
and his first act was to replace Byroade in Cairo and
transfer Allen.

To the well informed, this was a clear portent of
things to come, and the London *Times* made the
changes its main lead-story the next day. But after seeing the cotton lobby men, Dulles decided it would be
convenient to make the warning to Nasser even more
explicit. The same afternoon he telephoned the President
to get his agreement to scrap the Aswan project.
Eisenhower, who was playing golf, and whose interest
in the dam was, to say the least, dispassionate, told

Dulles to go ahead. So the die was cast, and the first step taken towards the Suez catastrophe.

* * *

The American decision took London by surprise. True, neither Sir Anthony Eden nor the Foreign Office had ever liked the Aswan project. Their economic experts considered it unsound and unlikely ever to be completed. Mr Selwyn Lloyd, the Foreign Secretary, had regarded Nasser as a national enemy ever since March, when Nasser, or so he thought, had engineered the dismissal of General Glubb, Britain's 'strong man' in Jordan, and had timed it to coincide with Lloyd's State visit to Cairo. He was not enthusiastic, therefore, about a project which would undoubtedly strengthen Nasser's régime. Still, along with the other members of the Government, he regarded the British contribution as an example of the danegeld which the West would have to pay, in ever-increasing quantities, to keep the 'neutralist' nations out of the Soviet orbit. Moreover, since December, the British Government had regarded the matter as settled. Sir Anthony Eden, therefore, was put out when Mr Dulles telephoned him on Wednesday July 18 to announce that he was withdrawing American aid the next day. But he had no choice except to follow America's lead. On Friday afternoon, Mr Selwyn Lloyd announced the British withdrawal to a half-empty and apathetic House of Commons. 'We came to the conclusion', he said,

> 'that the Egyptian Government would no longer be in a position to devote to the dam project the degree of priority necessary to secure its success.'

As has been shown, the British Government came to no such conclusion. It came to no conclusion at all. It played no part in the first move of the Suez drama. The responsibility was exclusively American.

*   *   *

Press comment was divided. *Time* magazine, forced to make a snap judgment just before going to press, hailed the Dulles withdrawal as a decisive move. It was, said *Time* approvingly, 'a gambit that took the breath of professionals for its daring and won the assent of kibitzers for its instinctive rightness'. The London *Times* was more cautious; it accepted the governments' reasons as valid, but added that an alternative scheme for the Nile waters should be 'reconsidered'. Some British Leftist papers were openly critical, while the *Economist*, writing more in sorrow than in anger, said that 'they [the British and American governments] cannot congratulate themselves on a brilliant stroke of policy'.

*   *   *

Cairo's reactions were swift and momentous. Nasser had built his mass popularity on two castles in the sky : a war of annihilation against Israel and the Aswan Dam. He returned from Brioni, dazed with glory, having wined and dined on a footing of equality with the world's two top neutralists, to find one of his castles snatched away. To Selwyn Lloyd Aswan was a bag of danegeld; to Dulles it was a pawn in his battle with the Senate; but to Nasser it was life or death. The project, drawn up in October 1955 by a team of British engineers, aimed at conserving 32,000 million cubic metres of water annually by creating a vast reservoir stretching over 739 square miles. It would have enabled

Egypt to bring under permanent cultivation 2 million additional acres of land, to make accurate crop forecasts, and to double her electricity supply. Since Nasser had ousted General Neguib, his régime of young officers had concentrated almost entirely on building up a strong army. Beyond reducing corruption at the top governmental level, and redistributing a few thousand acres of land, they had done virtually nothing for Egypt's 10 million *fellahin*. Their invariable reply to criticism was: Wait for the Aswan Dam. The dam was not merely four miles of concrete; it was the future of Egypt—and the future of Colonel Nasser.

Now the dream had vanished. Or had it? Nasser's first move was to get on the telephone to his ambassador in Moscow. The previous autumn, Russia had criticised the conditions laid down by the West in return for their loans as 'imperialistic', and had offered to finance the dam herself. But her offer—couched in vague terms—smelled suspicious, and Nasser had wisely preferred to turn to the West. Now, in desperation, he appealed to Russia. But Moscow had other things on its mind, notably trouble in Poland. It shared, moreover, the doubts of Mr Dulles' advisers as to Egypt's capacity to carry the project through. Finally, it calculated that an enraged Nasser might prove a serious embarrassment to the West. It decided to let things ride. On Saturday July 21, Mr Shepilov, the Soviet Foreign Minister, announced that Russia would, of course, be only too willing to assist Egypt in any way it could. But, he added innocently, Russia was not 'at the moment' considering financing the Aswan Dam.

Nasser saw clearly that the project was now doomed.

But he could not admit as much to the Egyptian
people. Nor could he allow what was manifestly a
deliberate slap in the face by Britain and America to go
unpunished. His first act—aimed at the U.S.—was to
recognise Communist China, thereby breaking his word
to Byroade. But this was not enough. Searching desperately for a gesture spectacular enough to reassert his
crumbling prestige, his eye fell on the Suez Canal. On
Sunday afternoon he asked a group of legal and engin-
eering experts, led by Mohammed Badawi, to draw up
plans for seizing and nationalising the Canal in the
following week.

The committee reported back on Tuesday. Since the
Canal Company was Egyptian, they said, to nationalise it
was an act of sovereignty which could not be challenged
under international law. They brought with them the
text of a nationalisation decree, a suggested list of
Egyptian directors to replace the officers of the old
company, and emergency plans for assuming operational
control of the Canal. They had worked fast and well.
On Thursday afternoon Nasser struck. Egyptian security
police, armed with the decree, took over the headquarters of the Canal Company, and informed its
employees—mainly British and French—that if they
refused to carry on working they would be liable to
prison sentences of from three to fifteen years.

The same evening, at a mass meeting in Alexandria,
Nasser announced the news to a screaming, hysterical
crowd of 100,00 Egyptians. Sweating under the arc-
lights, gripping a microphone with both hands, he spoke
for two and a half hours, reviewing the whole of
Egyptian foreign policy since the régime came to power,

and screaming, as the climax to his speech, that Egypt
would take the revenues of the Canal to pay for the
Aswan Dam :

> 'Americans, may you choke to death on your fury!
> The annual income of the Suez Canal Company is
> $100 million. Why not take it ourselves? We shall
> build the high dam as we desire! The Canal Com-
> pany shall be nationalised. And it will be run by
> Egyptians! Egyptians! Egyptians!'

The crowd swayed and chanted with frenzy. 'It was like
watching', said one observer, 'a dæmonic sorcerer
conjuring up from the bowels of the earth the legions of
hate and fury.' Across the vast continents of Asia and
Africa hundreds of millions of coloured men stirred.
Three thousand miles away, in Djakarta, the Indonesian
Government repudiated its debts to Holland. In
Damascus, the Secretary of the Syrian Chamber of
Deputies asked all Arab countries to nationalise the oil
companies operating on their territories. Across the
Middle Eastern land mass, the fate of £10,000 million
Western investments was at stake.

Chapter Two

THE SPECTRE OF MUNICH

SUEZ! TO THE old imperialist Powers of the West, the name was like an incantation. To France, the Canal was the greatest single masterpiece of Gallic ingenuity, the gloriously fulfilled dream of her finest engineer, Ferdinand de Lesseps. It was a tangible monument to the image of his country which lies deepest in every Frenchman's heart—*la France civilisatrice*. It was more than this; with its headquarters in Paris, its board controlled by French directors, its staff recruited mainly from French technicians, its shares held by tens of thousands of French *petits épargneurs*, it was the last great international stronghold of French capital. North Africa was in flames, the frontiers of the French Union were everywhere retreating, France was a poor, defeated, struggling country, forced to beg for American dollars, but Suez—*le Suez*—was a reminder of the magisterial past.

And Britain? To Englishmen, Suez was the clearing-house of Empire, the narrow channel through which the troopships sailed to conquer Kabul and Mandalay and Kuala Lumpur. Kipling had sailed through it, and Roberts and Curzon and Kitchener. It was the road to India and the fabulous treasures of the East. Through its great camps at Moascar and Ismailia, millions of

British soldiers had passed in two world wars. And Suez was Disraeli : the master-stroke of Britain's greatest imperial statesman, who, in one historic evening, had astonished the world with his cunning and revealed to Europe the irresistible power of the Pound Sterling.

Across these two countries, painfully readjusting themselves to the values of the twentieth century, earnestly, slowly and, in part, successfully coming to terms with a world in which 'colony' was a dirty word, historic memories stirred. But if the first reaction to the Suez seizure was a clutch of emotion at the throat, an atavistic surge of the past, there was a more sober and hard-headed response. To nineteenth-century Britain, striding the sea-lanes and the world, and splashing whole continents with the red of empire, Suez was vital; but it was even more vital now. On the morning of Friday July 27, while the Foreign Office was desperately signalling its Atlantic allies, the British Treasury experts were hard at work totting up the consequences in terms of sterling and barrels of oil. It soon became clear that the situation was grave indeed.

A few figures sufficed to show that Nasser had Britain by the throat. The year before 14,666 ships had passed through the Canal, of which 4,358 were British, representing over a quarter of the total tonnage. Moreover, these ships included tankers transporting nearly three-quarters of Britain's oil supplies. If shipping through the Canal were interrupted, Britain would have to reimpose petrol rationing within a week, and industry would be seriously affected within a fortnight. The long-term consequences were even more serious. Britain was now planning for an annual 3 per cent increase in her standard of living; the controlling factor in this increase was our ability to raise power output. For every 1 per cent increase in living standards, power consumption had to rise by 0.7 per cent. This meant, in concrete terms, that by 1985 fuel consumption would rise to 430 million tons of coal or its equivalent. Until atomic power was available in large quantities—and this would not be for another twenty years—a great part of this huge increase would have to be met by oil imports, which, by 1985, would reach 90 million coal-equivalent tons a year. We couldn't afford to pay for this oil in dollars. That meant we had to get it from the Middle East. And that meant we had to get it through the Suez Canal. The Canal, in short, held the key to the whole future prosperity of Britain.

What if the Egyptians refused our ships passage—as they had already done to the Israelis for three years? Then our tankers would have to go round the Cape of Good Hope. But this meant an extra two weeks on the journey, and a 30 per cent rise in transport costs. Besides, there weren't enough tankers. World demand for oil was increasing so rapidly that all tanker shipyards were booked up until 1960. Only three shipyards in the world could build the giant, 100,000-ton tankers which alone could make the Cape route a serious proposition. And the cost? Unbelievable. To carry 100 million tons of oil from the Persian Gulf to Europe via Suez required 14 million deadweight tons of tankers. To carry the same quantity via the Cape would require an extra 7.5 million deadweight tons, which would cost £500 million to build. And this only to meet present needs; if we were forced to go on using the Cape route, we should have to double our tanker fleet every ten years. The result? A steep and continuous rise not only in the price of petrol, but in the price of all goods produced by oil-consuming industries.

And what if Nasser allowed us to continue to use the Canal—but on his own terms? He would certainly raise the dues, which already averaged £8,000 a ship. Moreover, since he proclaimed that Aswan would be financed from the Canal dues, he would be forced to cut down on capital investment. The available profits of the Canal were not, as he stated, $100 million, but a mere $30 million; the rest went to the operation, maintenance and enlargement of the Canal. If this money were diverted, the Canal would soon break down. Even as things stood, the Canal was rapidly becoming out of date. The old company's plans to increase its capacity to forty-eight ships a day, due for completion in 1960, were already outstripped by the increasing flow of traffic. By 1965, making the fullest allowances for projected improvements, the Canal would reach its maximum capacity of 100 million tons of crude oil a year. But by that date, western Europe would be importing nearly 200 million tons a year. How was it to get through? The obvious—and cheapest—answer was to build pipelines, both overland, through Syria and the Lebanon, and alongside the Canal itself. There was also a plan for a duplicate Canal, which would cost £120 million and take eight years to complete. But the capital for these projects would have to come from the West; and, if Nasser were allowed to get away with his grab, this capital would not be forthcoming.

Nor was this all. If Nasser gave the lead—and went unpunished—would not others follow? What about the giant British-dominated Iraq Petroleum Company, and the Kuweit Oil Company, which, together, produced

more than two-thirds of Britain's oil? If they were
nationalised, their new owners would, presumably, continue to supply us with oil—but they might not be willing to let us pay for it in sterling. Arabs prefer Cadillacs
to Austins. And what would we do then? Our balance
of payments problem—which all our most heroic efforts
since the war had failed to solve—would then become
so grave that we should have to reduce imports not
merely of films and tobacco but of essential industrial
commodities such as wood and steel.

In other words, if Nasser blocked the Canal, Britain
would face the worst industrial crisis in her history. But
even if he allowed our ships to go through—but
remained in full possession—we might be forced not
merely to forgo our plans to double our standard of
living within a generation, but even to lower it below
its present level. Aswan was Egypt's future. The Canal
was Britain's.

Doubtless the information available to Sir Anthony
Eden that hot summer evening contained only the gist
of the above facts; but it was sufficient to sound the
alarm. Indeed, it may, perhaps, have been too alarming.
A wiser voice might have reminded Sir Anthony that
Britain stood on the edge of the Atomic Age; that Calder
Hall was nearing completion; that within twenty years
cheap, abundant and *home-produced* fuel would be freely
available. Arab oil would be indispensable to us only for
the next two decades, and if we played our cards skil-
fully we could keep it flowing. Why all the fuss? Why
not allow Nasser to keep his canal and come to some
working arrangement with him? What was wrong with
paying the sheiks a little more danegeld? After all, this
was the principle on which Aramco, the American com-

pany in Saudi Arabia, had always worked, and Aramco had never experienced the slightest trouble. A little tact —and not too much pride—could keep things jogging along for the next twenty years, and after that the Arabs could be told to go and drown themselves in their oil.

Wise counsel. But the Treasury did not supply it. The Treasury, in fact, was already in a state of turmoil. It had just been reorganised and given a long-term economic planning department. It was inclined to be long-term minded, in a slightly hysterical way. And the fact that the new department was still in process of settling itself down and anxious to take the first opportunity to exert its authority and influence, did not help matters. Nor was Sir Anthony the man to take Treasury alarmism with a pinch of salt. Sir Anthony has had a distinguished career as a Foreign Secretary, he is an able parliamentarian, a gifted speaker and an accomplished linguist; but not even his warmest admirers would call him an economist.

* * *

Besides, there were other considerations. Nasser's seizure of the Canal was not an isolated outrage; it was the culmination of a long, systematic and vicious campaign against British interests in the Middle East. Britain's connection with the area, as Sir Winston Churchill was to write some weeks later, was 'a long and honourable one'. It was certainly long. In the wake of Allenby's army, sweeping up the eastern littoral of the Mediterranean in the closing months of the first world war, came a whole generation of British administrators, soldiers and Arabophiles. After the British Army had left, they had remained. From the wreckage of the Ottoman empire they had carved out a series of kingdoms: the mandated territory of Palestine, Transjordan, Iraq. The operation was designed to secure the overland route to India, and to seize the oil resources of Mesopotamia. To accomplish it, we formed an alliance with the great dynasty of the Hashemites, which claimed the right to protect Mecca, and the suzerainty of Arab and Bedouin tribes from the Mediterranean to the Gulf. To three of its members we gave kingdoms, and protected their interests by supplying British political advisers, British officers and British gold. In return we expected obedience and oil.

For a whole generation we got both. The Arab leaders, who had fought alongside us against the Turks, formed bonds of friendship with their British masters. It was a friendship based on mutual self-respect and self-interest. But by the end of the second world war, the old generation had begun to die. Hussein of Iraq was the first to go. Then Abdullah of Transjordan, killed by the bullet of an anti-British assassin. Our old friend the Shah of Persia had resigned in 1941, and his faithful lieutenant, General Razmara, was killed in 1952. By the beginning of 1956, the only survivor was General Nuri Said, Prime Minister of Iraq. The new generation did not regard us in the same way. To them, we were not friends and companions-in-arms, but uninvited foreigners, unctuous, hypocritical, self-righteous, grasping, restraining their newly discovered nationalist spirit. They were growing up, and we were their parents, blindly regarding them still as children. The new mood was not confined to the ruling class. British organisation had brought law and order, a rising birth-rate, prosperity and with it a middle class. We chose to ignore these merchants and clerks and intellectuals; for the

seconded British officer or the Foreign Office official,
brought up on *The Seven Pillars of Wisdom*, the Arab
was a noble man-child, riding a white horse across the
desert wastes, lying, disobedient perhaps, but docile and
governable in knowing hands; he was not an urban
creature, interested in newspapers, oil revenues and
democracy.

This was our first error. Our second—inevitable perhaps—was that, in making the Hashemites our friends,
we had made the Saudis our enemies. The Saudis, like
the Hashemites, claimed Mecca; and, despite the British,
they had made good their claim by force of arms.
Unlike the Hashemites, moreover, they had made themselves independent. Throughout the Arab world they
were able to put forward their claim to leadership not
merely on dynastic grounds but on grounds—now infin-
itely more compelling—that they were the sole force
capable of freeing the Arab peoples from British tutelage.

Throughout the inter-war years, the Saudis intrigued
against us, mining away from within our puppet
Hashemite kingdoms. But in those days they were poor,
backward and impotent. Then, in 1946, came oil.
Aramco, backed by Standard Oil of New Jersey, the
world's biggest oil company, began to exploit the eastern
littoral of Saudi Arabia. Within five years, it was found
that the country had the biggest proven reserves of oil
in the world, and Aramco was paying King Saud
$500 million a year for the right to extract it. This was
money not merely for Cadillacs and refrigerators, but
for anti-British subversion. It poured into Syria, Iraq,
Jordan. Some trickled into Aden and its protectorates,
and into the British-run sheikdoms on the Persian Gulf.

Yemen and the vast desert of Oman were brought into the Saudi power *bloc*.

Then, in 1952, the Saudis found a new and powerful ally: Egypt. Egypt was, in many ways, the most advanced of the Arab countries, and potentially the most anti-British. The destruction of her monarchy unleashed the potent nationalist forces stirring within it; and when General Neguib, who bestrode the nationalist tiger for a time, was replaced by the younger and more forceful Colonel Nasser, the transformation was complete. Nasser was the son of a poor assistant postmaster in a Nile village. His political education had taken place in the streets, among gangs of youths rioting against the British. He was knowledgeable, after a fashion, clever and eloquent. His *Philosophy of the Revolution*, a hastily written rag-bag of philosophy, sociology and history, rapidly became a textbook of Arab nationalism, a handbook for Arab discontent throughout the area of British and French political domination.

Nasser's first achievement was to eject the British forces from the Canal Zone in 1954. He thereby removed the principal obstacle to a renewal of the Arab-Israeli conflict, which had smouldered since the armistice of 1948. Next he set about welding the Egyptian Army into the most potent military force in the Middle East. It took priority in the budget; under its new commander, Nasser's friend Abdel Hakim Amer, it acquired modern organisation on British lines, and a trickle of modern arms, mainly from Britain and France. Cairo became the centre of hope for Arabs throughout the Middle East, both for a victorious renewal of the conflict against Israel and for the ejection of the British. After 1954, Nasser became the host of exiled politicians

from Algeria, Tunisia and Morocco, and even from
Syria and the Lebanon. He sent out his own emissaries :
lawyers and political technicians, to Jordan and Iraq, to
Aden, to the Gulf. Everywhere they organised nationalist
political movements, and subversion against the British
and the Hashemites. The Saudis, recognising their new
ally, linked their gold to Egyptian know-how. The Arab
world began to polarise between Baghdad, now the
centre of Hashemite power, and Cairo. In 1955, Egypt
formed an 'action pact' with the Saudis. This was followed by a joint command of their forces, under
General Amer; soon Syria and Yemen joined in. In
September 1955, Nasser produced his master stroke : the
arms deal with Russia. Now, for the first time, he was
militarily independent of the West, and could acquire
arms in almost unlimited quantities and on long-term
credit.

Meanwhile, British policy was responding slowly and
disastrously. Britain, under the Balfour Declaration of
1919, had committed herself to the creation of a Jewish
'National Home' in Palestine. Nobody realised at the
time—or even later, when the promise, after much
prevarication and double dealing, was finally fulfilled—
the extent to which it would earn us the hatred of the
Arab peoples. But it was explicit, and Ernest Bevin,
despite his anti-Semitism and his vanity, which made
him fall an easy victim to the Arabophiles of the Foreign
Office, was obliged to subscribe to the principle of an
Arab-Jewish partition of Palestine when the British
withdrew. But, in the withdrawal itself, the ambivalence
of British policy reasserted itself; we failed to find a
settlement before we left, and the Arabs and Israelis
fought it out among themselves. The Israelis won—

against the hopes of the British Government, but with massive support from British and American Jewry. By the Arabs, the West was held responsible for Israel's survival.

After 1948, the fatal ambivalence continued. In 1950, together with the French and the Americans, we signed the Tripartite Declaration, a promise—deliberately vague—to come to the aid of whichever party to an Arab-Israeli dispute was attacked first. But no steps were taken to create a tripartite police force for this purpose, or to force the Arabs to recognise the 1948 armistice frontiers—which they had since repudiated—or to push a United Nations settlement. A U.N. Commission, with a small staff, was provided to investigate frontier incidents, but it was given no sanctionary powers. When, in 1952, Egypt refused to allow Israeli ships to pass through the Suez Canal—a flagrant breach of the 1888 Convention, which guaranteed freedom of passage —Israel appealed to the Security Council; Britain, France and America voted in Israel's favour but refused to implement their decision. On no less than 200 occasions between 1948 and 1956 the Arab-Israeli dispute was brought before the Security Council. On each, the Council, largely under British influence, refused to take any effective action. British policy, throughout these years, consisted of four words : preserving the arms balance. This meant, in practice, selling limited quantities of arms to both sides—an exceedingly profitable occupation. After September 1955, when Egypt and Syria got access to Iron Curtain arms, the balance was upset. But Britain refused to restore it. On no less than seven separate occasions the Parliamentary Labour Party pressed the British Government to send modern defensive weapons to Israel to counter the threat of Soviet MIG 15 fighters, Ilyushin bombers and heavy Stalin tanks. Each time it met with an outright refusal. Not only this: in January 1956, the Labour Party asked the Government to set up an international force in the eastern end of the Mediterranean which would be capable of implementing the Tripartite Declaration. Mr Selwyn Lloyd, Foreign Secretary, refused on the grounds that such a force was neither necessary nor opportune. Throughout the spring and summer of 1956, it became increasingly obvious that Israel would be forced to unleash a preventive war before Arab superiority in modern weapons became decisive.

Britain's refusal to act was based on grounds of self-interest. Anything we did to help the Israelis—and to impose a peace settlement would be construed as such—weakened our position in the Arab world. At the same time we could not stand by and watch Israel destroyed. The ambivalence of our Arab-Israeli policy affected our relationships with countries throughout the area. In the years following 1948, Britain had no Middle Eastern policy. British oilmen, exploring the resources of the Persian Gulf, complained bitterly and often of the lack of a firm British line; Saudi imperialism, they maintained, was encroaching on the loosely defined interior frontiers of the oil-bearing sheikdoms and protectorates, and Britain was doing nothing in reply.

The change came in 1952, when Dr Mossadeq nationalised the vast refinery of the Anglo-Iranian Oil Company at Abadan. Britain was unable to intervene in force, for fear of a Russian reprisal in northern Persia; and in the subsequent settlement our interests lost heavily to the Americans. Afterwards, the oil lobby

2—TSW

faction in the Foreign Office got the upper hand over
the Arabophiles. British policy became more forceful.
Under the aegis of anti-Communist 'peripheral' strategy,
we created the Baghdad Pact, which completed the
polarisation of the Arab world, and which formalised
for all time the position of the Hashemites as British
stooges.

From then on, events moved rapidly towards a trial
of strength between Britain and Egypt for supremacy in
the Arab world. In September, Nasser got his first shipments of Czech arms. The same month, we supported,
before an international court in Geneva, the rights of the
Sultan of Muscat and Oman to the Buraimi Oasis,
occupied by tributaries of the Saudis. The court sus-
pended its sittings in confusion, and a month later we
resorted to force : the Sultan's army, staffed by British
officers, seized Buraimi. With Buraimi, the communications centre for the south-east Arabian interior, in our
hands, we could set about occupying the whole of
Oman; and in December, in a sharp, brief campaign,
the operation was completed. Meanwhile, British
bombers and fighter-bombers were attacking tribesmen
in the interior of the Aden Protectorates, 500 miles to
the south-west.

We had resorted to force; Egypt and her allies
responded. Then, in December, Britain made a fatal
mistake. Turkey, Pakistan, Persia and Iraq had already
joined the Baghdad Pact. We wanted Jordan too. But
Jordan, whose Palestinian west was scattered with Arab
refugees, anxious only for the resumption of the war
against Israel, and bitterly hostile to the British, was
divided. In one of the supremely foolish decisions of
postwar British policy, we sent General Sir Gerald

Templer, the 'strong man' of Malaya, to Amman, to persuade the Jordan Government into joining. He failed, and in failing earned this country the hostility of the young King Hussein and his advisers. It was a decisive step. Three months later, King Hussein, reading a copy of the British weekly *Illustrated*, saw an article entitled 'Glubb Pasha, Uncrowned King of Jordan'. General Glubb was a British officer, seconded to Jordan to command the Arab Legion, the two-division force which kept the ramshackle kingdom together. He was the King's adviser and tutor, and it was the power and authority of his force which kept a pro-Hashemite Government in power. He was, as Hussein was later to discover, his best friend; but, in a moment of childish anger after reading the article, Hussein ordered his dismissal. Effective power in the army—and hence in the whole kingdom—was handed over to representatives of a 'Free Officer Corps', a collection of discontented junior officers, pro-Egyptian and anti-British, who modelled themselves on the Nasser group which had seized power in Cairo.

Jordan was now effectively outside Britain's grasp—despite the three British airfields within its borders, and despite the annual subsidy Britain paid to balance its budget. Nasser was jubilant. The news reached Cairo during a dinner party on the banks of the Nile, given in honour of the visiting British Foreign Secretary, Mr Selwyn Lloyd; Lloyd was informed by telegram immediately after dinner, and he must have concluded that Nasser had timed the *coup d'état* as a deliberate insult. A week later, visiting the British-protected sheikdom of Bahrein, his car was stoned by Nasser-incited mobs, demonstrating against the unpopular local British adviser,

Sir Charles Belgrave. Another personal insult organised
by Nasser? Meanwhile, Nasser was completing his
military arrangements with Syria, Yemen and Saudi
Arabia, stepping up his campaign of hate and border
raids against Israel, and buying ever-increasing quantities
of Communist equipment. In April, he announced a
projected visit to Moscow, and a few weeks later he
informed the Jordanian Government that he would be
willing to replace the British subsidy from Egyptian
funds, provided the Jordanians flung out 'the rem-
nants of British colonialism', and joined his military
pact.

This was the situation in the last week of July 1956.
Egypt was financing and encouraging a deliberate,
systematic and increasingly successful campaign against
British interests in the Middle East. And her leader was
conducting it in a manner which gave offence to a
number of sensitive British politicians. The issues were
sharp and personalised.

*   *   *

A third factor must be taken into account in explain-
ing the British reaction to the seizure of the Suez Canal :
the past career, personality and character of Sir Anthony
Eden, Knight of the Most Noble Order of the Garter,
and Prime Minister of Great Britain. Sir Anthony was
the son of an eccentric Yorkshire baronet. He had
received a conventional English upper-class education :
Eton, Christ Church (where he took a First Class in
Oriental Languages), the King's Royal Rifle Corps
(where he served with distinction). The ablest of his
generation had been killed in Flanders; he soon won
preferment in the Tory Party. Baldwin made him

Foreign Secretary at the early age of thirty-eight. Two years later he resigned, ostensibly in protest against Chamberlain's policy of appeasement to the dictators. He was later to derive great kudos from this resignation; it brought him into alliance with Winston Churchill, who made him Foreign Secretary in his war-time Coalition Government and who designated him as his political heir when he finally retired in 1955. Eden was regarded as one of the heroes of Munich. In fact, he was nothing of the sort. He was certainly one of the architects of the whole policy of appeasement, and his eventual resignation—only under severe pressure from his Parliamentary Secretary, Lord Cranborne, later Marquess of Salisbury—was largely on personal, not policy grounds. He objected to Chamberlain's habit of conducting foreign policy without consulting him, as Foreign Secretary (a fault to which, as subsequent events were to prove, he was not immune himself). In any event, he did not draw the logical consequences of his resignation, and speak and vote against the Government; on the contrary, he was one of its most docile supporters.

It is possible that, in later years, as events proved the fallacies of the Munich policy, Eden reproached himself for not opposing it more actively. In this, he had a great deal in common with many other Tory politicians. Munich has left a scar on the Tory Party, a scar which will not heal until a new generation takes over. Many of its members, believing that the second world war could have been prevented if Britain had opposed the dictators earlier, vowed that their party would never again be guilty of such moral weakness. Eden was foremost among them. Gradually they succumbed to what

might be called a 'Munich psychosis', with a resultant
tendency to draw false analogies from contemporary
facts. As 1956 wore on, and the latent conflict between
Britain and the Nasser régime became more explicit, the
Tories, led by Eden, placed a tragic misconstruction on
Nasser's position and aims. Nasser was a dictator. His
Philosophy of the Revolution was an Arab version of
Mein Kampf. He preached violence and vaunted aggression. On the basis of these superficial similarities, they
deluded themselves into believing that Nasser was a
potential Hitler, whose dreams of conquest would
eventually plunge the world into war unless the democracies took resolute action before it was too late. The
fact that Egypt was a small, backward country, incapable of defending itself, as events later proved, from the
assault of tiny Israel, was brushed into the background.
The spectre of Munich was more substantial than facts.

Nasser's seizure of the Canal brought the psychosis
into play. This was the march into the Rhineland, 1936;
the point of no return. If the democracies failed to act
now, it would be too late. Something clicked in Sir
Anthony Eden's Munich-conditioned brain. Nasser had
committed 'an act of aggression'. The response was
automatic : he must be overthrown, to save the peace of
the world.

Now Sir Anthony was a very experienced international statesman. How did he fall into this childish
and lamentable error? It is possible that, in normal
circumstances, he would have seen the Canal seizure in
its proper international and historical context, and acted
accordingly. But these were not normal circumstances.
History shows that wars are created not by strong men
but by weak men; not by confident men but by desper-

ate men. And, at the end of July 1956, Sir Anthony's political position was not merely weak but desperate. He had taken over the premiership from Sir Winston—after admittedly nerve-racking delays—in most auspicious circumstances. The 1955 budget had distributed largesse to wide sections of the population, and almost immediately afterwards Sir Anthony had dissolved Parliament and achieved the distinction—unique in the twentieth century—of leading his party back to Westminster with an increased majority. It was in many ways a personal victory; a photograph of Sir Anthony, gazing stern but kindly, into a prosperous future, and captioned with the words *Working For Peace*, had proved the most successful election poster for many years. During the summer of 1955, Sir Anthony enjoyed a support among his own party such as even Sir Winston had never commanded.

Disillusionment set in almost immediately. During the summer, there was a marked strengthening of inflationary trends, discernible for the past four years. The balance of payments position deteriorated sharply. In October, Mr Butler, who had, it was said, opposed Eden over the electioneering budget of the spring, was forced to present an emergency budget, severely restricting credit facilities. There was widespread grumbling among the Tory middle class. There were rumours, too, that Eden was proving hopeless in Cabinet. He could never come to a decision. Why were the major Cabinet changes, expected ever since the election, so long delayed? Was it because Sir Anthony, who had always played a very junior role under Sir Winston, was incapable of assuming command? At the beginning of January the storm broke. The *Daily Telegraph*, normally the most austere and faithful supporter of Tory governments, published a vicious attack on the Prime Minister. It was Sir Anthony's habit, it wrote, when making public speeches to emphasise his points by smacking his fist in the palm of his hand; but the smack, curiously enough, was never audible. The article was entitled 'Waiting for the Smack of Firm Government'. Other Tory papers— the *Mail*, the *Spectator*—followed suit. The *Observer* reported widespread criticism among Tory M.P.s. The *Mirror* summed up Press comment in one gigantic headline: 'The Tories Say EDEN IS A FLOP'.

To what extent this Press campaign represented feeling in the country—and in particular feeling among Tory supporters—is debatable. Certainly, there was never any real danger of a parliamentary revolt against Eden's leadership, if only because there was no obvious man to replace him. Mr Butler probably summed up the feelings of most Tories when he referred to Sir Anthony with a trace of irony as 'the best Prime Minister we've got'. The Tories, of course, rallied round; and Eden got support from some curious quarters—in particular, Lord Beaverbrook, the arch-imperialist; his *Evening Standard* published a series of articles under the ludicrous title 'Eden is a *Good* Prime Minister'. But the effects of the campaign on Eden himself were immediate and catastrophic. From being essentially a moderate man, representing the political centre of gravity of the postwar Tory Party, he changed, almost overnight, into an extremist, searching the political horizons for an opportunity for displaying his powers of decision. He had always been petulant and irritable, inclined to sudden rages and fits of temper; his habit of slamming down the telephone was well known. Now he became a caged tiger, pacing up and down 10 Downing Street, and waiting for the signal to unleash 'the smack of firm government'. When he studied the text of Nasser's nationalisation decree, he did not for an instant doubt the moment had arrived. The general slide to anarchy in the Middle East, the alarm in the Treasury, the Munich psychosis merely confirmed his determination to act.

But Britain could not act alone. She needed allies. There were, alas, even more desperate men in Paris.

Chapter Three

THE WILD MEN IN PARIS

IF BRITISH POLICY towards the Arab world had suffered from ambivalence, in France there was no such ambiguity : by July 1956, France was at war with the Arab world. Inland from the 2,000-mile coastline of the Mahgreb, the western sector of the old Mohammedan empire, the flames of violence flickered and smouldered.

France had entered North Africa in 1830, when Marshal Bugeaud descended on Algeria with 200,000 men. In 1881 Jules Ferry extended her hold by establishing a protectorate in Tunisia. Finally, in 1912, Marshal Lyautey began the conquest of Morocco. After them came hundreds of thousands of French settlers, who built roads and ports and railways, established industry, broke up the feudal Arab estates, and planted vines and olives. By 1945, there were more than 1,500,000 of them, stretched from Casablanca to Tunis, Frenchmen by blood and education, North Africans by birth. Beneath them—apart from a handful of wealthy caids, reviled by their compatriots as French puppets and popularly known as *beni-oui-ouis*—was a vast *lumpenproletariat* of 20 million Arabs.

But in 1945, in the wake of the liberating Allied armies, came the seeds of a new era. Roosevelt instructed his local representatives, such as Robert Murphy, to encourage Arab leaders to secure self-government. There was an immediate response. Before the year was out, the Algerians revolted at Sétif, massacring the local French community. The French exacted a fearful penalty: Senegalese troops were told by their commanders to shoot, on sight, all adult male Arabs for the next twenty-four hours. More than 45,000, including many women and children, were murdered.

For the next ten years, throughout the Mahgreb, the sickening pattern was repeated again and again: Arab demands for self-government, blind French refusal, violent revolt, brutal repression. Moderate Arab leaders —those who advocated a dual, Franco-Arab community —saw their political power undermined by French in-transigence, and their followers desert to the advocates of violence. The extremist parties—the Istiqlal in Morocco, the Messalistes in Algeria, the Néo-Destour in Tunisia—gradually became dominant in the nationalist movements.

Successive French governments passed measures of constitutional reform; in each case they were sabotaged by the local French *colons* and their associates in the North African civil service, army and police. The Statute of Algeria, passed by an overwhelming vote of the Assembly in 1946, was never fully applied; and the elections for which it provided were faked by the local authorities—only *beni-oui-ouis* were returned. Tunisia was given a measure of self-government, including a cabinet, appointed by the Resident-General from among Arabs regarded as 'reliable'; but when even these proved unco-operative, in 1952, the Resident promptly dissolved the Government, without reference to Paris; the French Foreign Minister, Robert Schuman, was subsequently forced to endorse the act by pressure from the *colon* lobby in the Assembly. The next August, in Morocco, a conspiracy of *colons* dethroned the legitimate Sultan, Mohammed V, and replaced him with a French puppet called Ben Arafa; again the Foreign Minister, Georges Bidault, was obliged to endorse the *fait accompli*. By the end of 1953, the upland areas of both Tunisia and Morocco were in a state of permanent revolt, while the big cities were dominated by rival gangs of gunmen : Arab terrorists on the one hand and French counter-terrorists on the other, working in league with the local police, and murdering not merely Arab nationalists, but responsible and moderate Frenchmen who advocated a peaceful settlement.

In August 1954, the French Left made a last, des-perate and, in part, successful attempt to break out of the pattern of violence. Mendès-France, exploiting the vast popularity he had won in France by his successful solution to the Indo-China war, flew to Tunis and opened negotiations for a wide measure of self-government. The attempt appeared to have succeeded; negotiations towards a semi-independent status for Tunisia were carried on throughout the autumn; the Tunisian rebels were amnestied and ceased fighting; something approaching calm descended on the Mahgreb. Then, on the night of All Saints' Day, November 1 1954, the 'activist' wing of the Algerian Messalistes broke away from the leadership and launched a violent revolt in the Aurès Mountains in south-east Algeria. They appeared to be well armed and organised. Pre-liminary attempts by the French Army to suppress the revolt were unsuccessful. Fighting settled down for the winter, and the revolt began to spread to other areas in

Algeria. Mendès-France's majority in the Assembly declined abruptly, and at the beginning of February his Government collapsed.

He was succeeded by Edgar Faure, a wily professional politician whose own views were progressive, but who was dependent for support on a Right-Centre majority. Despite the pressure of the *colon* lobby, he managed to complete the negotiations for the new constitution of Tunisia; but in Algeria he was forced back on to a policy of blind repression. More and more French troops were moved into Algeria. Then, as spring turned into summer, the situation in Morocco deteriorated sharply. The almost universal hatred with which the Moroccans regarded the French puppet sultan, Ben Arafa, had been compensated, in part, by his alliance with El Glaoui, the last of the great feudal Berber chieftains, who controlled most of the southern Atlas. But El Glaoui's power was now beginning to collapse : the revolt against French rule was spreading even to his own tribesmen.

On August 20, the second anniversary of the deposition of the legitimate sultan, the tribesmen rose in revolt, not only on the Moroccan side of the Atlas but to the east, in the mountains of western Algeria. Over 2,000 French *colons* were massacred. The next day, the French Army and Air Force moved in. Whole tribes and villages were destroyed. The total number of Arabs killed—men, women and children—will never be ascertained, but it is believed to be in the region of 60,000. Those who escaped joined the rebels in western Algeria, or a new organisation, set up in the Atlas, called the Moroccan Liberation Army. Morocco itself was now ungovernable, and in October El Glaoui abruptly changed sides and renewed his allegiance to Mohammed V. This was decisive, and immediately afterwards the French Government removed Ben Arafa to Tangier and restored the legitimate sultan. Before he returned to Rabat, the capital, he demanded and obtained a preliminary agreement which granted Morocco semi-independent status. It went much further than the Tunisian treaty, and Habib Bourguiba, the Tunisian Prime Minister, promptly requested equivalent concessions for Tunisia. It was rapidly becoming clear that both Tunisia and Morocco were lost to French rule.

But what of Algeria? The fighting had grown fiercer throughout the summer and autumn; goaded by repression, more and more young Algerians were joining the rebel bands; they supplied themselves with captured French arms and a trickle of munitions from Egypt, which were smuggled across the Libyan frontier; gradually the insurrectionary areas spread and linked up. But until the end of 1955 there was still a chance for a negotiated settlement. Moderate Arab leaders refused to join the rebels and condemned their excesses; a substantial section even of the *colons* believed that a new statute could be devised which would give the Algerians a real share in the government of the country and yet protect the interests of the French minority. Messages sent out from rebel-occupied areas indicated that they, too, were prepared to compromise.

This was also the mood of metropolitan France. In December, harassed from all sides, the Faure Government collapsed and promptly dissolved Parliament. In the subsequent election campaign, fought over Christmas, Mendès-France's Radicals linked forces with the French Socialists in a coalition called the Republican Front, and fought the election almost exclusively on a programme of negotiated settlement in Algeria. The French electorate responded. The Socialists, Radicals and Communists—who also favoured negotiation—each gained substantially in votes. The members of the Faure coalition lost heavily. When Parliament reassembled at the end of January, the Republican Front found itself in command of a working majority, pledged to negotiate peace in Algeria.

Then the first difficulty arose. Who was to be Prime Minister? Mendès-France was the natural choice. He enjoyed immense personal popularity among progressive Frenchmen of all parties. He was identified with the policy of reform in North Africa. And he was a man of unshakable determination, against whom the pressures of *colons* and generals would prove useless. Unfortunately, the party he led, by virtue of numbers, was the junior partner in the coalition. Guy Mollet, General Secretary of the French Socialist Party, had the first option on the premiership. Despite the entreaties of his own colleagues, he refused to decline it.

It was Mollet's first senior governmental appointment. Since 1946, he had controlled the machinery of the Socialist Party, basing his power on two big federations in the north of France, which, together, enabled him to command a majority at party conferences. He was an expert manipulator of the block vote, a superb intriguer in the *couloirs* of the Assembly, a back-stairs politician, with a long and distinguished record for overthrowing France's transient governments. But he had never held supreme power himself; and he was a vain and timid man. The Government he formed consisted mainly of his own nominees in the Socialist Party, and two or three Right-wing Radicals, themselves political

opponents of Mendès-France. Mendès-France was made
a Cabinet minister without portfolio; the only other
member of the Government with a progressive record
on North Africa was Alain Savary, Minister for Tunisian
and Moroccan Affairs.

Mollet's first move—in accordance with the electoral
programme of the Republican Front—was to fly to
Algiers and begin negotiations for a peace settlement.
Before leaving Paris, he had appointed General Catroux,
a well-known progressive, Governor-General in Algeria.
But the day after Mollet arrived, whilst he was laying a
wreath on the war memorial in Algiers, his party was
attacked by a mob of 20,000 hysterical *colons*. For
Mollet, it was the moment of truth; his first contact with
the realities of government. His face and clothes spat-
tered with rotten eggs and tomatoes, he was carried,
trembling and almost unconscious, into the offices of the
Government-General. His first act was to telephone Paris
and cancel Catroux's appointment; instead, he designated Robert Lacoste, a Cabinet minister known to
favour the *colons*. His next act was to return to Paris.
The electoral promises were forgotten. The negotiations
were abandoned. And the only alternative was to carry
on the war.

For a few weeks, Mendès-France remained in the
Cabinet, trying desperately to brake the drift to catas-
trophe. Then, abruptly, he resigned in disgust. Hence-
forth, a group of four men controlled the Government.
There was Mollet himself, rejoicing in a new-found
popularity among the Right and Centre of the Assembly.
There was one of his placemen, Christian Pineau, the
Foreign Minister, a Right-wing Socialist who wrote

children's fairy stories in his spare time and who indulged in Napoleonic day-dreams. There was the Defence Minister, Maurice Bourgès-Maunoury, a Right-wing Radical who was the Government's contact man with the *colon* lobby in the Assembly. And finally there was Lacoste, who was given a rapturous welcome when he arrived in Algiers, and who promptly pledged himself to a military suppression of the revolt.

But how? By the beginning of March, France had 250,000 troops in North Africa. A preliminary assessment by the general staff in Algiers concluded that the revolt could be contained, and eventually stamped out, if the available forces could be increased to 400,000. Similar assessments had been produced, at intervals, throughout the long and disastrous course of the Indo-China war. But Lacoste had never fought in Indo-China. He forwarded the report to Paris with his enthusiastic approval. The Cabinet adopted it. Legislation was drawn up, and passed, for the recall of 150,000 reservists and for the assignment of additional military credits from the budget reserve. Throughout the spring, more and more men were shipped to Algeria. There was widespread opposition. Whole regiments of reservists mutinied. Troop-trains were derailed. An entire shipload of reservists broke loose in Marseilles and hid themselves in the Old Port. There were violent incidents at Paris and Le Havre. Nevertheless, the military build-up continued.

Lacoste had promised the Cabinet a 'dramatic improvement' in the military situation by the beginning of May. May came and went. Military headquarters in Algiers stepped up their claims of 'terrorists' killed and captured; but the area in the hands of the rebels continued to spread. In April, the revolt reached the hills overlooking Algiers and spread even into the suburbs of the capital. By May it had swept over the whole of western Algeria and was operating in conjunction with units of the Moroccan Liberation Army in the Atlas. The railway from Constantine to the Algerian south was cut and had to be abandoned. Larger and larger French units were ambushed by well-armed rebel bands. Locally recruited Algerian and Moroccan troops—and even Senegalese, sent up from France's central African colonies —proved increasingly unreliable; whole companies killed their white officers and deserted to the rebels. In May, Lacoste was forced to order the withdrawal of all non-French regiments from the fighting. In June, the rebels, now provided with an effective headquarters and a superb system of intelligence, switched their activities to isolated *colon* farms in the rural areas. The *colons* began to withdraw into the big towns, and there swell the chorus of criticism.

What was going wrong? Why had 400,000 men, with every advantage of modern equipment, failed to crush a rebellion which consisted of—as the French repeatedly claimed—'a handful of desperate murderers'? The facts were painfully simple. The prime nourisher of the revolt was French policy itself. Brutal repression was gradually driving the entire Algerian people on to the side of the rebels, and many of them into their ranks. The conduct of the French, throughout the rebellion, can only be compared to the barbarism of the Russians in Hungary. Villages known, or suspected, to be supplying the rebels with food were obliterated by jet fighter-bombers (supplied, incidentally, by American off-shore funds for

NATO defence against Russia); flame-throwers and gas bombs were used against mountain hide-outs. Torture was employed against prisoners; both *gonflage à l'eau*, the forcible injection of water by a reverse stomach-pump, and the notorious *ceinture éléctrique*, an electrical-shock device perfected by the Gestapo. By May, some 40,000 Arabs were interned in vast, filthy concentration camps outside Algiers. Liberal Frenchmen were expelled or arrested. Arab lawyers, doctors, teachers, who had played no part in the rebellion were given long terms of imprisonment, schools were shut down, newspapers suppressed, hospitals were handed over to the military. With each excess, each act of violence, more Arabs drifted into the hills, or joined the murder gangs in the towns. The Algerian Liberation Army, which had numbered a mere 3,000 at the outset of the revolt, had swollen, by May 1956, to nearly 100,000.

And it was becoming well armed, too. News of French arms convoys invariably reached rebel headquarters; they were often successfully ambushed and their contents captured. The native regiments, before their withdrawal, handed over their weapons freely— even artillery trains. French reservists, dragged from their homes to fight a *colons'* war, sold their arms in the big towns. An immense black market in deadly weapons sprang up in the native quarter of Algiers; by June, a sub-machine gun could be bought for £25, a rifle for £10; all were French army issue. Nor did the rebels lack for money. The *beni-oui-ouis*, enriched by grants of land and money from the French Government, were blackmailed by the rebels; they contributed freely to save their lives from sudden assassination. The money thus obtained bought more arms. As in Indo-China, the

French were not merely arming both sides; they were financing them too.

But none of this could be told to the French public. A scapegoat was required, an alibi for failure. The only answer was: Cairo. During the first half of 1956 all the Algerian leaders who had managed to escape death or imprisonment had fled there, where they formed the Committee for National Liberation. They were undoubtedly helped by the Egyptian Government with money and, to a certain extent, with arms. Some of these—a trickle—reached the rebels. On this flimsy basis the French Government constructed a vast campaign of hatred against Egypt, personalised in the figure of Colonel Nasser. The French Press and radio fell into line. But for Egyptian aid, it was said, the rebellion would collapse. Stories were circulated of vast quantities of Russian arms, transported into Algeria across the desert, or shipped into lonely creeks on the Algerian coast; Egyptian and Iraqi officers were said to be directing rebel operations; Egypt's role in Algeria was identical to that of Communist China in the Indo-China war.

To what extent did the Government believe its own propaganda? It is difficult to say. Certainly they accepted the view of the military commanders, who advanced Egypt as an excuse for their own failures. Pineau, the most gullible of the four principal ministers, undoubtedly placed responsibility on Egypt. Early in the summer, he paid a visit and extracted—so he told the Assembly—a promise from Colonel Nasser that he would cease aiding the Algerians forthwith. What exactly occurred during this conversation will probably never be known. It is highly unlikely that Nasser made any such promise; but Pineau, in his muddled way, believed that he had; and when, as the weeks went by and brought no improvement in the military situation in Algeria, Pineau concluded that Nasser had broken his solemn word of honour. Nasser had also made him look ridiculous in the eyes of the Assembly. By June, Pineau shared with Selwyn Lloyd a growing animosity towards the Egyptian dictator. About this time, he ordered the Quai d'Orsay to open up private negotiations with the Israeli Government. Hitherto, France, like Britain, had supplied arms to both sides in the Arab-Israeli dispute; but from now on supplies to Egypt were cut off, and those to Israel substantially increased.

The other three ministers did not completely share Pineau's illusions. But they agreed with him in seeing Egypt as the key to a solution in Algeria. Mollet was in favour of opening negotiations with the rebels as soon as the military reinforcements had brought an improvement in the situation. Lacoste—backed by Bourgès-Maunoury—rejected this argument as unrealistic. There might be, he said, some improvement by the end of the year—but not before. In the meantime, it was essential to shake the confidence of the Algerians in their ability to eject the French by force of arms. And this could only be done by striking at Egypt. Nasser had made himself the champion of the Arab world; in recent months he had gone from success to success. If his bubble could be pricked, if the reality of his power could be exposed—and by France—then the psychological effect on the Algerians would be decisive. At the moment, France could only negotiate from weakness; but if Nasser were destroyed or tamed, she could negotiate from strength.

Through May, June and July, the debate continued in the French Cabinet. Gradually, Lacoste's argument carried the day. Gradually, French ministers came to regard the real enemy as Nasser and not the Algerian rebels. Only the opportunity for a showdown was lacking. And a showdown was becoming more urgent. The Mollet Government, elected to make peace in Algeria, had chosen instead to carry on the war on an ever-increasing scale. But despite the flood of men and material flowing into North Africa, despite the daily communiqués of rebel groups 'annihilated', the French public was becoming increasingly aware that the war was being lost. The bills, too, were coming in. At the beginning of July, Paul Ramadier, the Minister of Finance, made a report to the Cabinet which revealed that France—after four years of financial stability—was poised on the verge of a fresh wave of inflation. If the retail price index rose by a further 0.2 per cent, all French industrial workers would become automatically entitled, under the sliding-scale wage-price agreement, to wage increases of 5 per cent. Moreover, he added, if the war continued on its present scale beyond October, it would be necessary to revise the budget estimates and introduce massive increases in taxation.

Two weeks later, Nasser seized the Canal. The opportunity had arrived. Here was the gratuitous insult, the long-awaited signal for the campaign of retribution. The next day, an excited Pineau was on the telephone to 10 Downing Street.

Chapter Four

THE FRUSTRATED INVASION

SOME TIME ON Friday July 27, Sir Anthony Eden spoke to M. Pineau on the long-distance telephone. The conversation, it now seems, revealed one salient fact: their mutual determination to take swift, decisive and military action against Egypt. Nasser, they decided, must be overthrown, and the only speedy and practical manner in which this could be accomplished was by the threat—or use—of force. At this stage, neither minister can have had full consultation with his Cabinet; neither had examined the legal position resulting from the Canal seizure; neither had consulted with their NATO allies or with representatives of the other maritime powers whose interests were involved in the Canal; nor had Sir Anthony spoken to the Commonwealth Prime Ministers. Above all, neither had been provided with information as to the military possibilities of an armed descent on Egypt. Nevertheless, both agreed to act; and the same evening, in Paris and London, the Defence Ministries were alerted. This telephone conversation set the pattern of precipitous, ill-informed and irresponsible decision-making which was to be the hallmark of both governments throughout the crisis.

The next morning, there was swift disillusionment. In Paris, MM. Mollet and Pineau received a brief report

from the Ministry of Defence which revealed a grave
state of unpreparedness. A section of the Mediterranean
fleet was at Toulon and could be ready to move within
forty-eight hours; but its solitary carrier was equipped
with only twenty-five modern planes capable of fighting
on approximately equal terms with Nasser's Russian-
built MIG 15s and 17s. The fleet could not be in the
eastern Mediterranean in less than a week. There were
three active squadrons of Mystère-4 long-range jet
fighters in Germany, but it would take ten days or more
to transport them and their maintenance equipment to
the Mediterranean; in any case, they would be useless
if based in Algeria; the farthest point from which they
could hope to operate was Cyprus. All France's remaining jets were too short-ranged even for this. As for
ground forces, there were three infantry battalions in
barracks in the Algiers area, and two more on the
French south coast; but they had no landing craft of
any description. Two brigades of paratroops were
already engaged in Algeria; they had received, moreover, no parachute training for over a year, and would
certainly need a fortnight's re-training. Troop transport
planes could be provided, but it would take some time.
As the morning wore on, it became rapidly evident that
France was materially incapable of taking forceful action
by herself against Nasser.

The news in London was even worse. As the *News
Chronicle* revealed in a striking article on October 31,
we had three parachute battalions in Cyprus; but they
also had had no training for months; since no parachute
training-chutes were available in Cyprus, the men would
have to be flown back to Britain for re-training. There
were eight infantry battalions in Cyprus, but not one

solitary landing craft; the nearest supporting artillery
was in Germany. Part of the 10th Armoured Division, it
is true, was scattered about Libya; but they also were
without tank transports. Scattered infantry battalions in
Aden and East Africa were equally stranded and
immobile. We had no modern long-range fighters any-
where in the Middle East or Mediterranean areas, and
only two active squadrons of Canberra bombers—both
based on airfields in Arab countries which would certainly forbid their use for operations against Egypt. The
Mediterranean fleet was available, but its carriers were
only equipped with obsolescent aircraft. Army transport
and dock specialists, essential for any sizeable amphibious
operation, were scattered all over the British Commonwealth. Above all, the decisive factor was tank landing
ships. A calculation showed that a force capable of
effecting a landing in the Canal Zone, and of defending
itself against the assaults of the Egyptian forces, would
require a minimum of seventy. We had precisely two;
the rest of our fabulous D-day armoury had been sold,
destroyed or allowed to rot in 'mothballs'.

By the weekend it was clear that the invasion was off
—or, rather, postponed; the determination of Sir
Anthony and his French allies remained unshaken.
Orders were issued in both capitals for emergency mobilisation plans—including the recall of reservists and the
re-activisation of reserve equipment—to be drawn up at
once. Meanwhile, time had to be gained. The military
preparations must, with all speed, be concealed behind
a smoke-screen of negotiation. What could the resources
of diplomacy achieve?

From a purely legal point of view, the picture was
dismal. In London, hasty legal consultations soon

Were there any other steps we could take? Colonel Nasser, by seizing the Canal without consultation, and by placing armed guards on the Company's property, had undoubtedly committed an unfriendly act—indeed, some might say an aggressive act. We had, therefore, some right to retaliate by imposing economic sanctions. This idea was first put forward by Mr Gaitskell, Leader of the Opposition, immediately after the seizure, and gratefully accepted by Sir Anthony (no doubt, he had already thought of it himself, but he was glad to have the suggestion come from the Opposition). But it was not, on closer inspection, a very effective form of retaliation. Egypt's sterling balances, amounting to some £120 million, were promptly blocked; but the next payment was not due, in any case, until December. The Government also froze all Egyptian trading and private accounts in Britain; but this was a step of the utmost gravity, which might irreparably damage world confidence in Britain as a central banker. It also affected Britain as much as Egypt; our exports to Cairo, both of manufactured goods and machinery, would be cut off. The Egyptian bourgeoisie, certainly, would feel the pinch; but not the mass of the Egyptian *fellahin*, on whom Nasser's power rested, nor, in the short run, the Egyptian economy as a whole. These steps, taken together, and in conjunction with corresponding measures in Paris, would freeze one-third of Egypt's currency reserves. This would cause some dislocation in Egypt's current trading, but would not, in itself, cut her off from world markets. During the last eighteen months, she had run down her reserves by 25 per cent, but she still held, at the latest count, some £E86 million reserves in gold and dollars, which we could not touch, even with American co-operation. Using 1954 figures as a rough basis for calculation, she could carry on for two years—even without assistance from the Communist *bloc*.

There remained diplomacy pure and simple—the massing of world opinion to force compliance on Egypt, or to provide a complacent background for armed intervention. But world opinion was divided. The Communist *bloc* and the nations of free Asia accepted, in varying degrees, the legality of Nasser's seizure. European opinion was highly critical, especially of the manner in which Nasser had acted, but it envisaged a diplomatic solution. The Netherlands—which had just lost £200 million as a direct consequence of the seizure—might have been prepared to go further, but the entire country was in a state of uproar over Queen Juliana's public quarrel with her husband; its Government was in no position to take dramatic decisions. As for America— the by-no-means-innocent cause of the whole affair— America was already absorbed in the Presidential election campaign. On July 27, Sir Anthony, it was said, experienced difficulty in getting any responsible American official on the telephone, and at Eisenhower's first Press conference after the seizure, Anglo-French correspondents had to wait for nearly an hour, while the President answered questions about his campaign, before being able to slip in a modest query about Suez.

It is possible, indeed, after three disheartening days of attempting to enlist world opinion on his side in favour of armed intervention, that Sir Anthony, if not M. Mollet, might have given up the whole plan in despair. But one thing encouraged him to go on : the apparent unanimity of opinion at home. The first Press reactions

to the Suez seizure had revealed a hitherto unsuspected
depth of hostility to Egypt, and those most clamorous
for strong action—the *Express*, the *Mail*, the *Telegraph*
—appeared to represent a very wide body of public
opinion. Even *The Times*, normally a cautious paper,
which had approved the 1954 Suez withdrawal,
vehemently demanded a firm line from Britain. For the
first few days, this mood appeared to be shared by a
large section of the Labour Party, and in particular by
its leaders—Mr Gaitskell, as we have seen, was the first
to suggest economic sanctions.

So we come to the fatal August 2 debate, the first
occasion on which the House of Commons had had an
opportunity to give full consideration to the implications
of the Suez crisis. I say fatal because it was on the basis
of this debate that Sir Anthony judged—wrongly as
events later proved—that the great majority of the
nation would support him in military action against
Egypt. Just after noon, in a crowded and excited House,
he rose to speak. He regretted, he said, that he could not
yet disclose the Government's intentions. Mr Dulles had
only arrived the day before, and talks with him and
M. Pineau were still in progress. Meanwhile, he reminded
the House of the grave threat to the British economy
which the Canal seizure represented. He referred to
Nasser's 'arbitrary action' in breaking treaties and international contracts; we saw now, he said, 'the nature of
the régime with which we have to deal'. In view of this,
we had decided to take certain military measures of a
precautionary nature, including the recall of 'a limited
number' of reservists, and the movement of certain units
to the Mediterranean.

It was, despite its underlying threat, a restrained

speech, certainly more restrained than the one from Mr Gaitskell which followed. Mr Gaitskell, it should be said at once, was in a difficult position. He had always been an economist, never an expert on foreign affairs; he tended to see the Suez crisis from an economist's point of view, and was correspondingly alarmed. In recent months, his speeches on the Middle East had been delivered after careful coaching from his colleague, Mr R. H. S. Crossman, who probably knew more about the area than any other member of the House. But on August 2, alas, Mr Crossman was not available, and Mr Gaitskell had to rely on his 'shadow' foreign minister, Mr Alf Robens. The result was disastrous. It is true that Mr Gaitskell ended his speech by suggesting that the dispute should be dealt with by the U.N., and by insisting that any action we took—and he did not rule out the possibility of force—should be consistent with our obligations under the Charter. But this appeared to be almost an afterthought, which followed a long review of the Middle Eastern situation. The seizure of the Canal, he said, was 'part of the struggle for the mastery of the Middle East'; prestige issues were involved. The pattern was 'very familiar. It is exactly the same that we encountered from Mussolini and Hitler in those years before the war'. If we failed to assert our rights our remaining friends in the Middle East would desert us and we should lose our oil. The tone of the speech— and this, rather than the references to the Charter, is what impressed the House and the Prime Minister—was one of restrained bellicosity.

But worse was to come. After a number of desultory speeches, including one from Captain Waterhouse, leader of the Suez Group, in which, with undisguised satisfaction, he congratulated Mr Gaitskell on his 'extremely courageous speech', Mr Morrison rose to his feet. Morrison had been Labour foreign secretary at the time of Abadan, and the criticism his handling of the crisis provoked had rankled ever since. His speech was a violent attack on Nasser—'that pocket dictator in Cairo' —and an apparent encouragement to the Government to use force, with the support of America and the United Nations if possible, but without them if need be. Government benches—if not all the Labour benches— greeted it with cheers, and Mr Selwyn Lloyd, who followed immediately afterwards, expressed his 'admiration' of the sentiments expressed.

It is true that some Labour members—in particular Mr Warbey—uttered a note of warning; others, such as Barbara Castle, planned to attack the whole principle of 'military precautions', but were unable to catch the Speaker's eye; but in general the Government cannot be blamed for assuming that the majority of the Labour Party supported its threats of force. And by the weekend, Parliament had dissolved and its members were scattered all over the country—indeed, all over the world. For the next month, Sir Anthony Eden was deprived of the vital sounding-board, the indispensable guide to public feeling, which the House of Commons, with all its faults, still constitutes.

*   *   *

Meanwhile, he and Mr Selwyn Lloyd, in conjunction with the French, set to work to prepare their diplomatic smoke-screen. By the end of the first week of August, it was clear that they could count on only lukewarm support from America. The day after the seizure, Sir Anthony had telephoned the State Department and requested that Mr Dulles should come immediately to London for three-Power talks. Mr Dulles had refused. He was too busy. Instead, he sent Mr Murphy, a comparatively junior official and a noted Arabophile; during the hurried weekend talks which followed, it became abundantly clear that Mr Murphy had no definite instructions and was not empowered to take decisions. On Monday, Anglo-French pressure on Washington increased, and Dulles reluctantly agreed to come over himself.

His arrival did not help matters. As a corporation lawyer, he naturally regarded Nasser's seizure of the Canal as a 'wrongful act'—but wrongful in a commercial sense. It could therefore be met by commercial sanctions—and he hinted that America was prepared to take similar steps to Britain and France in restricting Egyptian credit. He also thought that American ships should not pay Canal dues to Nasser's company, though he hastened to add that he could not issue instructions to this effect. In any case, he said, Nasser did not appear to be insisting on payment of the dues to Cairo—at least for the moment.

In general, Dulles gave Eden and Pineau an impression of confusion and irresolution. But on one matter he seemed clear. The dispute, he thought, should not be referred to the United Nations at this point. Recent additions to its membership, which raised the total to seventy-six, had, he feared, upset the old majority through which the Atlantic nations had controlled the U.N. General Assembly since the war. This must sooner or later become apparent. But it was important that it

3—TSW

should not first reveal itself on an issue such as this, which involved the interests of the big Western Powers all over the globe. At the same time, however, public opinion had to be mobilised against Nasser—then he would climb down. Far better, therefore, to call a conference of the States which used the Canal, or were economically dependent on it; this would give Britain and France what might be termed 'a majority mandate' in their negotiations with Nasser.

A sensible line of argument, from Mr Dulles' point of view. But Mr Dulles believed the dispute could be settled by negotiation and by diplomatic and economic pressure. Britain and France did not. They were already determined to encompass the fall of Nasser. This, they felt, could be brought about if Nasser was forced to capitulate over the Canal. For this reason the terms they presented had to be unacceptable to him. Inquiries in Cairo had already revealed that Nasser would not, under any circumstances short of force, accept a solution which vested the operational control of the Canal in the hands of an international body. This, therefore, was the solution they advocated. Mr Dulles also thought international control was desirable. But for him it was a basis for negotiation, a starting-point for protracted discussions. For Britain and France it was a minimum demand, which had to be accepted or rejected outright, a take-it-or-leave-it final offer.

Hence, although Britain and France fell in with Dulles' plan for a users' conference, their view of its purpose was entirely different. To him, it was designed to strengthen the hand of the Allies in the negotiations which, in his view, must inevitably follow. To them it was a means to secure general approval of an Anglo-

French plan which, if rejected by Egypt (as they had good reason to believe it would be), would be followed by armed intervention to secure compliance. It was also a convenient way of gaining time to prepare such intervention. By the end of the first week of August, it had become painfully and abundantly clear that an Anglo-French expeditionary force could not be assembled, in sufficient strength to make it immediately effective, before the end of the first week of September. The conference could not meet before the middle of August; it could be expected to last several days, perhaps longer. By the time it had drawn up its demands, presented them to Nasser, and had them rejected, the end of August would be reached. Britain and France would then refer the matter to the Security Council, where Russia would promptly use her veto. They could then claim that they had done their best to work through the U.N., but had been prevented, as so often in the past, by Russian sabotage; their only course, therefore, was to take action themselves. And by that time the expeditionary force would be ready.

In unison, therefore—but acting from very different motives—the three Western Powers invited the user States to a world conference. The guests were carefully selected to ensure a majority for the Big Three plan. Egypt and Russia could not, of course, be excluded; but all the rest were either members of NATO or METO or of the Commonwealth, or, as in the case of Japan, Spain and Ethiopia, economically dependent on the West. The jury was rigged—but not, as events were to show, sufficiently rigged.

Meanwhile, public opinion had to be prepared. In France, it did not need much preparation. When M.

Mollet, addressing the Assembly a week after the
seizures, described Nasser as a Hitler who had to be
destroyed, he was greeted with strident applause from
all the parties except the Communists. During the last
six months, as the fighting in Algeria had grown more
intense, public opinion had swung round behind the
Government; hatred of the Arabs was spreading among
all sections of the population, and there had been race
riots in several French towns.

In Britain it was different. Indeed, by the time Parliament had gone into recess, deep differences of views had
already begun to appear. A group of Left-wing Labour
M.P.s, led by William Warbey and Anthony Wedgwood
Benn, had already formed a Suez Emergency Committee, which planned to mobilise public opinion against
a war with Egypt. Mr Gaitskell was being attacked for
his attitude by Labour militants all over the country,
and by such papers as *Tribune* and the *New Statesman*.
Nor was anxiety confined to the Left. The *Observer*,
while deploring the use of force, thought this was not the
intention of the Government; but others were less
optimistic. The *Manchester Guardian*, in particular,
warned its readers in the strongest terms that a resort to
force would be disastrous. The *Economist*, too, under-
lined the weakness in law of the Anglo-French case,
and implored the Government to set about negotiating
in a realistic manner.

But the bulk of the Press was solidly behind the
Government. *The Times*, which at this stage influenced
the Government more than any other organ of opinion,
insisted that we be firm. The morning after the August 2
debate, its leading article was entitled 'Resisting the
Aggressor', and it hinted darkly of 'getting our foot in

the door'. In any case, the Government was rapidly committing itself. In radio-television broadcasts, both Sir Anthony Eden and Mr Selwyn Lloyd made personal attacks on Colonel Nasser, describing him in terms which made it perfectly clear that they had no intention of negotiating with him. More important still, before Parliament went into recess, Mr Selwyn Lloyd had spoken to Tory back-benchers at a private meeting of the Conservative Foreign Affairs Committee. What exactly he said we shall probably never know, but there is no doubt that he committed the Government to securing the internationalisation of the Canal at all costs. Tory M.P.s cheered him to the echo and went back to their constituencies well content. After that meeting, the Government —even had it so wished—could not retreat without imperilling its future. The decision was made. The next step was to lay the smoke-screen.

Chapter Five

THE DIPLOMATIC SMOKE-SCREEN

THROUGH THE WET, chilly days of August—it was the worst summer England had experienced for many years —the Foreign Office worked desperately to rally international support for the Anglo-French position. Every conceivable pressure and threat was exerted to bring our allies and dominions into line. A preliminary estimate revealed that only Australia and New Zealand were likely to stand by us if we took military action against Egypt, and even they were doubtful. The rest were suspicious and hesitant; India and Ceylon in particular were openly critical of Britain's bellicose attitude; whilst European countries such as Norway and Italy, though themselves economically dependent on Suez, refused to consider even the possibility of participating in an armed expedition.

Of the twenty-three nations invited to attend the conference, all—except Egypt herself—accepted; but many arrived in London with grave misgivings. Most of them, having a major economic interest in the Canal, were plainly anxious to see it well administered. They certainly agreed with Selwyn Lloyd when he deplored the possibility that this vital waterway might be subjected to what he called 'the transient impulses of a single military dictator'. But they would probably have been content with firm guarantees from Egypt, endorsed by the United Nations. None were in favour of using force which, apart from anything else, would endanger the Canal itself; and many objected to the way in which they were being marshalled into line to give backing to what they regarded as Anglo-French colonialism. By the time the conference assembled, diplomatic tempers were wearing thin.

In Cairo, Nasser remained cool and self-confident. Knowing that any assault on British lives or property would immediately be used as an excuse for intervention, he kept his mobs in hand. He withdrew his threat to imprison Company officials, such as pilots, who resigned; a number did so. The strain on those who remained increased, but they kept traffic moving. To avoid trouble, Nasser refused to respond to the provocative Anglo-French action in freezing Company assets in London and Paris and instructing their ships to pay dues only in London; he was prepared, he said, to accept this pending a settlement. Israeli ships were still refused entrance to the Canal; otherwise, he took infinite pains to uphold the 1888 Convention to the letter. It was plain he was getting good advice, though whether from the Indians, or the Russians, or both, it was difficult to say. He was also organising material assistance to meet the economic threat of the Anglo-French financial squeeze. In conversations with the Soviet Ambassador in Cairo, Kiselev, he arranged deferred payments on Russian imports and increased credit facilities. Saudi Arabia advanced $10 million for current trading; Syria agreed to supply 100,000 tons of wheat for payment in Egyptian pounds. Export firms in India,

Japan and West Germany, eager to enter a previous
British monopoly, offered goods on easy credit terms. By
the middle of August, it was becoming rapidly apparent
that Egypt could resist Anglo-French economic pressure
almost indefinitely.

The Universal Company had also been busy. For the
past two weeks, many of its permanent officials had been
commuting between Paris and London, seeing politicians
and diplomats. The central question was the position
of the Anglo-French pilots and technicians on the
Canal itself. Everyone agreed—erroneously as it later
turned out—that Egypt could not work the Canal
without them. The Company was anxious to withdraw them immediately; so was the French Government. But the British advised caution; the time
for that would come later—after the conference,
and after Nasser's rejection of its terms. Meanwhile, the
Company prepared the way, instructing its employees
that, if they left the Zone, they would be retained on full
salary and allowances pending a settlement; but that
their departure should be delayed until further instructions were received. It was also active in French newspaper offices. Cheques for undisclosed sums were
privately sent to Paris dailies, enclosed in a letter
thanking them for their presentation of the Company's
case, and referring to a 'contribution' towards 'expenses'.
Unfortunately, one of these cheques—for the equivalent
of £100—was sent to the fellow-travelling *Libération*,
which had been uniformly hostile to the Company since
the crisis broke, and which now promptly published the
letter and cheque, in facsimile, on its front page. The
secret was out, and the other newspapers published
statements that they had refused to accept the money.

Against this background of intrigue and counter-intrigue, the conference opened. The venue chosen was Lancaster House, off the Mall, and into its Long Gallery, a smallish, blue-and-gold salon, hot and stuffy at the best of times, a vast throng of ministers and diplomats were squeezed. Every effort was made by the Foreign Office to keep the Press at a distance. They were forbidden access to Lancaster House itself, allegedly because they would trample its valuable carpets, and pushed into a temporary Press house set up in Carlton House Terrace. There they were regaled, at intervals, with meagre progress reports, read out by Sir George Young, head of the Foreign Office News Department, whose manner seemed assertive and, in the eyes of most of the foreign journalists present, to personify the entire British approach to the problem. Attempts to interview individual delegates, in order to ascertain their views and intentions, were discouraged and, if possible, prevented.

Nevertheless, it was soon apparent that the conference was not going well. Eden and Pineau had persuaded Dulles to act as Western spokesman, and to present the international control plan to the conference. But according to French Press reports, he insisted that the plan be watered down. The name of the international body was changed, first from 'Authority' to 'Board', and finally to the 'Suez Canal Office'. Even so, it got a mixed reception. Most of the Commonwealth and west European nations appeared to approve it, but Persia and Pakistan were hesitant. Spain produced a compromise plan, suggesting a joint Egyptian-international board, with a court of appeal in the event of disputes. The Indian delegate, Mr Krishna Menon, rejected the plan outright, as being incompatible with Egyptian sovereignty.

Instead, he produced an alternative plan, which provided
for an international *advisory* board, and a new version
of the Convention, which Egypt would be required to
sign and which would be made subject to United Nations
sanctions. It was, looking back on it, a sensible plan,
because it did not infringe Egypt's sovereignty and at the
same time protected the interests of the user States; for,
if Egypt violated the new convention—and there was no
reason to suppose she would wish to do so—they could
take action under the U.N. There was no doubt that a
majority of the conference would have been prepared to
accept the Indian plan; so, in all probability, would
Egypt. But for this very reason it was violently rejected
by the British and French. The Menon plan opened the
way to a negotiated settlement; and what they wanted
was not a negotiated settlement but a military showdown
with Nasser.

Nevertheless, Krishna Menon, despite Anglo-American
pressure, refused to withdraw his plan. It had been
hoped, originally, that the conference, with the exception of Russia, would be unanimous. Now, there was
nothing to it but to take a vote (though even here,
Britain, who controlled the conference's secretariat,
refused to use the word 'vote', just as later she refused to
use the word 'war'). Seventeen nations, marshalled into
line by Mr Selwyn Lloyd and Mr Dulles, supported the
American plan. Spain supported her own. India, Russia,
Ceylon and Indonesia supported the Menon plan.

The next stage was to present the majority plan to
Cairo. When the conference ended, a transcript of its
proceedings was duly dispatched to Nasser. But a more
positive form of drawing his attention to the conclusions
of the conference was required. At this stage, Mr Dulles

put forward a suggestion that a sub-committee of the conference be formed to take the plan to Cairo. The British and French agreed, with the important proviso that the sub-committee should be empowered merely to argue the merits of the plan and should not be permitted to present it as a basis for negotiation. Dulles, anxious to get back to Washington, accepted the proviso : a fatal mistake. The scheme was, accordingly, adopted, and 'Burly Bob' Menzies, the Australian premier, was chosen as chairman of the delegation, which included representatives of four of the States which supported the Dulles plan.

Hence the conference ended on a note of ludicrous unreality. Menzies was to go to Cairo to present a plan which he knew perfectly well Nasser would reject outright. He had no mandate to negotiate. All he could do was to note Nasser's refusal and return to London. What would happen then? To whom was he to report? The conference did not decide. Nothing was decided. And this was fully in accordance with Anglo-French wishes. From the outset, they had regarded the conference merely as a means of erecting a background of international support, against which they could take whatever action they thought fit. They did not want the conference to take decisions. They intended to take the decisions themselves.

*　　　*　　　*

Meanwhile, emphasising the threat behind the Menzies mission, military preparations continued on an ever-increasing scale. In the first half of August, some 25,000 reservists were recalled. Landing vessels, tank-carriers, destroyers, minesweepers were taken out of mothballs. At Catterick and Salisbury, tanks, lorries, T.C.V.s and Bren-carriers were painted desert yellow. Long convoys began to wind their way to ports on the South coast. Troop transports and naval units steamed towards the Mediterranean from all corners of the globe. Canberras and Hawker Hunters were flown out from Germany. A vast armada was collected at Malta; an infantry division was flown out to Cyprus in the biggest air-lift since the Berlin blockade.

The French, too, were preparing. In the Algiers region, elements of three divisions—one armoured— assembled. Six infantry battalions were encamped near troopships at Marseilles. While Menzies was preparing to set out for Cairo, a statement was issued simultane- ously in Paris and London, announcing that 'to ensure, in case of need, the protection of French nationals and their interests in the eastern Mediterranean', France had been granted permission to station 'certain forces' in Cyprus. In Cairo, Nasser announced that Egypt would 'resist invasion by all possible means' and ordered general mobilisation.

In Britain, the news that French forces were to land in Cyprus—confirming rumours that a full-scale invasion force was being assembled in the island—served to widen the split in public opinion. The Press was now bitterly divided; the *News Chronicle*, the *Herald*, the *Man- chester Guardian*, the *Observer*, the *Mirror*, bitterly attacking the war preparations—now personally identi- fied with Eden—while the *Mail, Express, Telegraph* and *Sketch* applauded. *The Times* was behaving in a peculiar manner. Its leader on August 3 entitled 'Resisting the Aggressor' had dismissed the legal aspects of the Canal dispute as mere 'quibbling', which, it claimed, would 'delight the finicky and comfort the faint-hearted'; it had, as a result, been criticised in the strongest terms by Sir Frederick Leith-Ross, one of Cromer's successors in Cairo, and by Sir Ralph Stevenson, until recently Ambassador to Egypt. Its author, *The Times* foreign editor, Mr MacDonald, appears to have had second thoughts afterwards and to have revised his opinion. Unfortunately, early in August he went on holiday, and Sir William Haley, the editor—whose journalistic activities had been previously (and wisely) confined to the book page—took it upon himself to write leaders on Suez. As a result, the day the London conference opened, *The Times* astonished its readers with a leader entitled 'Escapers' Club', which accused those who criticised the Government's stand of being interested only in Diana Dors and Test matches—'escapists' in short—and called for a sense of 'greatness' and 'adventure'. The unfavourable response this lamentable epistle evoked was, happily, so overwhelming that thereafter the paper began to change its line. By the time the Suez invasion was actually launched, it was openly critical of the Government, and a week afterwards it felt itself able to write that '*The Times* has never concealed its misgivings about this enterprise'.

There was a similar, but more rapid, change of front in the Labour Party. The uneasiness expressed by a few Left-wing back-benchers during the August 2 debate spread swiftly to the movement as a whole. Impromptu meetings organised by the Suez Emergency Committee all over the country attracted surprisingly large audiences; public opinion was mobilising. On August 7, a letter published in *The Times*, signed by Mr Denis Healey and Mr Douglas Jay, and written, it was believed, with the knowledge of Mr Gaitskell, indicated that the Party leadership was becoming alarmed. On August 13, the Labour Party shadow cabinet felt itself obliged to issue a statement drawing attention to the references to the United Nations in Mr Gaitskell's August 2 speech. The next day, its members called upon the Prime Minister and asked him to issue a statement indicating that the Government was not preparing to use force in a manner inconsistent with the U.N. Charter. Sir Anthony refused. This was an historic decision : it meant that bi-partisan foreign policy, one of the dominant factors in British politics since 1945, was at an end. From this point on, a recall of Parliament became inevitable. The only question was : when? For two weeks, Eden adopted delaying tactics. Then, abruptly, he gave the word. Parliament was recalled in special session for September 12.

By this time, however, the invasion force was ready. A joint Anglo-French staff was already working together in Nicosia and its commander, General Sir Charles Keightley, had been designated. By this time, too, Mr Menzies, after five fruitless days in Cairo, had returned to London angry and empty-handed. D-day was drawing near.

Yet the invasion did not take place. It was delayed for a further seven weeks. Why? For the answer to this question we must examine the strange behaviour of Mr Dulles.

Chapter Six

THE DULLES DOUBLE-CROSS

PARLIAMENT WAS DUE to reassemble on Wednesday September 12. The Menzies mission had failed. The country was deeply divided. The Labour Party was concerned about the Government's intentions. Sir Anthony's first task, therefore, was to tell the Commons exactly what he intended. We must assume that by now, he and M. Mollet had made up their minds. Their invasion force was now ready. Their first action, then, would be to withdraw all the Anglo-French pilots and technicians from the Canal, thus, as they believed, disrupting its service. Once traffic had begun to slow down, they would immediately appeal to the Security Council. Russia would block the Security Council's motion by using her veto. Thereupon, the British and the French, having, as it were, 'squared their yard-arm' with the U.N., would be able to occupy the Canal Zone, quoting as their authority the 1888 Convention. That, in brief, was the Anglo-French plan, and by Monday morning, September 10, Eden had presumably already drafted a Commons statement based on this assumption.

But on Monday, it appears, he received a telephone call from Mr Dulles. What followed should be a warning to all future members of the Foreign Service never to conduct diplomacy by telephone. Ever since the end of

67

the London conference, Mr Dulles had been brooding over the way the French and the British had been behaving. He had also been reading newspaper accounts of the military build-up in Cyprus. He was, in short, becoming suspicious. Were they intending to 'go it alone'? If so, he, Mr Dulles, must stop them. The Administration of which he was a member had been elected, in 1952, on a peace policy—'end the war in Korea'. It was shortly due for re-election. If, in the meantime, a war broke out in the Middle East, the Administration's electoral chances would suffer and he, Mr Dulles, would get the blame. He would, in fact, be out of a job.

But how to stop the British and the French? Obviously, they must be offered an attractive alternative. At this point in his ruminations, it appears, Mr Dulles sat down and, with the most perfunctory consultation with his advisers, drew up the famous plan for the Suez Users' Association. As he envisaged it, the user States were to club together, employ their own pilots (presumably the Anglo-French ones), pay their own dues to themselves and make their own way through the Canal. If Nasser refused to co-operate with the Association, they would then boycott the Canal, and—this was the bait for the Anglo-French—America would foot the bill. After a few months of this, Mr Dulles assumed, Nasser would be prepared to compromise. It does not appear that Mr Dulles worked out the plan in detail, or that he calculated—in the event of Nasser's refusal to co-operate—how much his scheme would cost America, or even that he studied the constitutional mechanism whereby Congress could be persuaded to provide the money. He simply got on the telephone to Eden.

What transpired in the course of this conversation, and in a further one the next morning, will probably never be known. Whether the confusion which subsequently arose was Dulles' fault, or Eden's, is equally obscure. Both men were undoubtedly in a state of nervous excitement. Mr Dulles is not noted for his lucidity at the best of times, and on this occasion we can safely assume that he was more than usually incoherent. But whoever was to blame, the indisputable fact emerges that Eden got the wrong end of the stick. He saw the green light ahead; his doubts were removed. America had capitulated. She was right behind the British and the French. She had agreed to form a Users' Association which would shoot its way through the Canal; and if anything went wrong, America would pay. The aura of Anglo-American amity had never hovered quite so perceptibly over 10 Downing Street as it did on the evening of September 10 1956.

Eden's first move was to inform the French; his next, to tear up his prepared statement and write another. In the next twenty-four hours, the Foreign Office and the Quai d'Orsay worked feverishly to prepare the details of the Association. The next afternoon, at three-thirty-eight precisely, a radiant Prime Minister rose to address the House of Commons. At considerable length, he reviewed the course of the crisis; he reminded members of the grave issues involved. Then he came to his point : America, Britain and France had decided to set up a Canal Users' Association. The details, he said, had yet to be worked out, but he could now give the House a broad outline of the scheme :

> The Users' Association will employ pilots, will undertake responsibility for co-ordination of traffic through

the Canal, and, in general, will act as a voluntary
association for the exercise of the rights of Suez Canal
users. The Egyptian authorities will be requested to
co-operate in maintaining the maximum flow of traffic through the Canal. . . . But I must make it clear
that if the Egyptian Government should seek to
interfere—

Mr Harold Davies (Leek): Deliberate provocation.

The Prime Minister:—with the operations of the
association, or refuse to extend to it the essential
minimum of co-operation, then that Government will
once more be in breach of the 1888 Convention.
(Hon. Members: 'Resign!') I must remind the House
that what I am saying—(An Hon. Member: 'What
a peacemaker!')—is the result of exchanges of views
between three Governments. In that event Her
Majesty's Government and others concerned will be
free to take such further steps—

Mr S. O. Davies: What do you mean by that?

The Prime Minister:—as seem to be required—

Mr Davies: You are talking about war.

The Prime Minister:—either through the United
Nations or by other means, for the assertion of their
rights. (Hon. Members: 'Oh!')

In conclusion, Eden added that he was writing a letter,
in conjunction with the French Government, to the
President of the Security Council, informing him of the
situation. He sat down amid deafening cheers from
the Conservative benches, and shouts and booing from
the Opposition.

Mr Gaitskell's reply was a brilliant—and, in other
circumstances, devastating—exposure of the weakness of

the Association. But so far as the Tory benches were concerned, it fell on deaf ears. They were not interested in whether the Association would work or not, whether, in practice, you could navigate one of the world's most difficult narrow waterways without controlling the service and signal stations ashore. All they knew—or cared about—was that we were going in to Suez, and that the Americans were going in with us. (As one Tory member put it: 'We'll send a battleship in at the head of each convoy!') Sir Robert Boothby wound up the first day of the debate, at nine-thirty that night, with a rollicking display of knock-about oratory which perfectly expressed the joy and relief the average Tory member was feeling. He ended:

'As I listened to the Prime Minister this afternoon, I thought of what Nasser had been saying about what he was going to do to establish an Arab Empire from Morocco to the Persian Gulf, and how he was going to eliminate Israel altogether. That is all in his speeches, and in a horrible little book called *A Philosophy of Revolution* [sic] which is like a potted edition of *Mein Kampf*. As I heard the Prime Minister speaking, I said to myself, "Well, thank goodness, at any rate we shall not have to go through all that again", and we shall not.'

Sir Robert was wrong. Tory members had to go through all that again—and the very next day. While they were sound asleep in their beds, dreaming of empire, Washington was in a state of ferment. As the text of Sir Anthony's speech came through on the tape, the State Department rose in horror. What on earth had Dulles

promised? Senators and Congressmen got on the telephone. The President was alerted. Within a few minutes,
Eisenhower was speaking to Eden on the long-distance
telephone, and there was no ambiguity this time. When
the conversation finished, Sir Anthony Eden must have
been a shrunken man. It was all a horrible mistake. The
aura of Anglo-American amity abruptly vanished. Dulles
had double-crossed him again. Moreover, this time it
was impossible to keep it a secret; at that very moment
Dulles, now in a state of ultimate confusion, was telling
a Press conference in Washington that he knew nothing
about an idea of shooting up Suez—all he'd thought
about was going round the Cape. As members filed into
the Chamber to take their seats for the second day's
debate, the text of Dulles' statement was ticking through
on the House of Commons tape machine.

By the middle of the afternoon, Tory back-benchers
were in a state of bewilderment and rising anger. So,
for that matter, was the Cabinet. Its members had
always been divided over Suez. A majority, led by Eden,
Selwyn Lloyd, Macmillan and Salisbury, were in favour
of strong measures. Others, such as Heathcoat Amory
and MacLeod, were doubtful. Butler and Monckton
were allegedly in favour of negotiation. Unfortunately,
at the first Cabinet meeting after Nasser's seizure, when
the basic decision was taken to make a stand, Butler
was away on holiday and Monckton was absent with a
tummy upset. Now, however, they were back, and acidly
critical of their colleagues. What, they asked, had Eden
got them into? He had committed the Government to
forceful action without first making sure that he had full
American support. Surely he knew Dulles well enough
to realise that nothing he said could be relied on—even

if it were down in writing? What were they supposed to do now?

Back-benchers were equally critical. A group of them —fifty or more—met in the Lobbies and decided to warn the Government that they could not support action which was independent both of the U.N. *and* America. Sir Lionel Heald, an ex-Attorney-General, was chosen to speak on their behalf. He rose at just after three-thirty. After stating that no responsible Government could give a guarantee not to use force under any circumstances, he went on to state that he, personally, could not support any action which involved a breach of Britain's international obligations. He then went on to quote the relevant sections of the Charter. Before resorting to force, he continued, we should be bound to refer the matter to the Security Council. This, he firmly believed, had all along been the intention of the Government, but in order to remove any ambiguity, he felt obliged to ask the Government to give a formal assurance to this effect.

It was a masterly speech. It demanded a plain—yes or no—answer. Immediately Sir Lionel sat down, Mr Gaitskell was on his feet. Eden was absent, brooding in 10 Downing Street; but Mr. Selwyn Lloyd was in his seat. Pointing his finger at the Foreign Secretary, Mr Gaitskell asked whether, in view of Sir Lionel's speech, he was prepared to give such an assurance. Amid a mounting chorus of booing from the Opposition benches, Selwyn Lloyd replied that the Prime Minister would deal with the matter when he wound up the debate.

The moment of decision had been postponed; but only for a few hours. By the time Eden rose to address the House, at nine-thirty, capitulation was written all over his sagging features. He was also in a raging temper.

But it was impossible to judge from his statement, what exactly the Government had decided. Mr Gaitskell therefore persisted with his questions. Was Eden prepared to say, he asked, on behalf of Her Majesty's Government, that they would not shoot their way through the Canal? Amid shouts of 'Answer!', Eden attempted to hedge. Finally, he admitted, to the accompaniment of Labour cheers, that if the Egyptian Government refused to co-operate with the Users' Association, he would take the matter to the Security Council. After this, there was nothing more to be said. The debate ended abruptly.

*   *   *

Eden's capitulation closed the first stage of the Suez Canal crisis. Whether by intention or by sheer good luck, Mr Dulles had succeeded in sinking beyond all hope of repair the original Anglo-French plan to invade Egypt on the issue of the Suez Canal. Eden had failed to get American backing for armed intervention; instead, he had found himself landed with Mr Dulles' absurd Users' Association, a scheme which he, Eden, had not invented and which he knew perfectly well was unworkable. But he was now committed to it—as the pages of *Hansard* testified. Not only was he committed to it, but, when it failed, as it undoubtedly would, he was committed to going to the Security Council. But he could not possibly retract everything he had said the day before. He had already eaten one and a half columns of *Hansard*; a further eleven and a half would be too much even for his digestion. Like it or not, the Users' Association was now the policy of Her Majesty's Government.

What, then, was he to do? The pilots had already

been withdrawn, and it was becoming rapidly clear that this, in itself, would not lead to an appreciable slow-down in traffic and so allow the Convention to be invoked. Thanks to Jugoslav, Greek, Russian and German pilots, hastily shipped into the Zone, and thanks to the efforts of their own pilots, who were working over-time, the Egyptians were taking ships through at the rate of thirty-six a day (the pre-nationalisation average was forty). The advantage of the Association, as Eden had hinted in his speech, was that it would force Egypt either to capitulate, or to refuse ships entry—and thus provide a pretext for force. But now, it appeared, the Association would simply re-route ships round the Cape. How many would agree to do so? The British and the French certainly; the Americans, too—if Dulles kept his word (but would he?). But the Norwegians, for instance? Why should they send their ships round Africa when the Egyptians had demonstrated that the Canal was still working? After all, they were not engaged in a personal trial of strength with Colonel Nasser.

The more Eden analysed the situation on the night of September 13, the more he was drawn to the inescapable conclusion : Nasser had won the battle for the Canal. On that issue at least, the French and British could no longer go to war.

But the Canal was not the only issue in which Nasser's personal prestige was involved. There was also Israel, and the patchwork of corrupt and crumbling Arab States which surrounded it.

Chapter Seven

THE PLOT IS HATCHED

WITH THE MILLSTONE of Mr. Dulles' ludicrous Users' Association hanging round his neck, Sir Anthony Eden plodded grimly on towards the diplomatic horizon. Anglo-French Suez policy was in ruins. The vast invasion force, collected in Cyprus and Malta, and growing daily, was—for the moment at least—useless. It could not now be employed on the Suez Canal issue. If the general situation in the Middle East developed 'favourably'— and Britain and France were now determined to make sure that it would—there might be an opportunity to use it later. Meanwhile, Sir Anthony was inextricably committed to a whole series of diplomatic steps which flowed inexorably from his disastrous statement of September 12.

First, the Users' Association had to be formed. The eighteen 'majority powers' of the first London Conference were unwillingly dragged back for another. As expected, it went wrong from the very first session. Most of the User States, who had somewhat grudgingly backed Dulles' internationalisation plan, were by now thoroughly alarmed, and highly suspicious of Anglo-French intentions. Pakistan, in particular, refused bluntly to partake in anything which remotely resembled a minatory gesture towards Egypt. Norway, Spain and Italy made it clear that they would not send their ships round the Cape so long as the Canal remained open. And Dulles was studiously vague as to the 'compensation', both in dollars and oil, which America would be prepared to pay if anything went wrong. The State Department, it is true, had by now drawn up an emergency plan to pool the resources of the American oil companies to provide emergency supplies to Europe; but it refused to divulge its details to the Foreign Office. Moreover, Mr. Dulles had now discovered that the plan would require not only Congressional approval but a waiving of America's anti-trust laws, on which Congress was particularly sensitive; it was evident, in short, that he would only be empowered to put the plan into action in the very gravest circumstances.

Hence, at the conference, he was able to offer only the meagrest comfort to Britain and France. He gave his general backing to the Canal Users' Association, but he was unable to guarantee that American ships would be forced to pay the Canal dues only to the Association's fund. At the end of the conference, he issued a statement that, on his return to Washington, 'steps will be taken with our Treasury officials, and with the representatives of American-flag vessels . . . with a view to perfecting this co-operation in terms of actual operating practices'. This vague phrasing meant, in practice, that the U.S. Treasury would refuse dollar licences for Egypt for shipping dues; but it was immediately pointed out in London that there were a large number of ways of evading this restraint, and that Mr. Dulles showed no particular determination to make his scheme watertight.

Other nations were even less willing to commit themselves on the matter of dues. Indeed, as the conference proceeded, it became clear that if Britain and France put forward a motion that all dues be paid to the Association, only a minority of the user Powers would vote for it. To avoid this open evidence of disagreement, no such motion was put forward. In short, the conference ended without settling the central issue for which it was convened : the payment of the dues. Its final declaration, vague to the point of meaninglessness, stressed the 'voluntary' nature of the Association; but even this could not be put to the vote.

This time, too, it was impossible to conceal the conference's total failure. 'Most people in this country', wrote *The Times,* 'will find it hard to know what to make of the London Conference and its results.' Hard indeed ! But the French were in no such difficulty. In his final conference speech, M. Pineau made it abundantly plain that he was bitterly disappointed by the conference's failure to take concrete and binding decisions, and he announced that France would adopt the final resolution only with 'the most express reserves'. The British Government felt exactly the same, but was unwilling to say so publicly. By this time, Mr Selwyn Lloyd and Mr Dulles were scarcely on speaking terms, and the day after the conference, September 22, Eden, Lloyd and Pineau met in private and decided to defy America's ban on an appeal to the Security Council. They announced their decision the next day—without previously warning Dulles—and a meeting of the Security Council was fixed for September 26.

So the diplomatic pantomime dragged on. The first meeting of the Association—a gathering at ambassadorial level—was arranged, and a Danish consul-general was appointed as its permanent administrator. Nobody told him what to do. Nobody was empowered to give him instructions. In any case, nobody had any idea what such instructions should be. Various pointless conferences —'at a technical level', as the Foreign Office put it— were held in London and New York. Meanwhile, the Security Council met in an atmosphere of some tension. Britain and France put forward a complaint against Egypt. Egypt put forward a complaint against Britain and France. The Council did agree, after some fumbling discussion, to put the British complaint first on the agenda. But a proposal by Jugoslavia—which, as an independent Communist State, objected strongly to Anglo-French colonialism—that both complaints should be discussed simultaneously, was only defeated by six votes to two, with three abstentions. Even the Western majority on the Security Council was showing signs of wear and tear.

When the Council met to debate the British and French complaint, Selwyn Lloyd's worst fears were confirmed. He had moved, at the outset, that the debate take place in secret session, and as soon as it opened Dr Fawzi, the Egyptian Foreign Minister, put forward a set of proposals which went very far towards meeting the Western demands, and represented real concessions on Egypt's part. It was therefore suggested that the time had now come when Selwyn Lloyd and Pineau should meet privately with Fawzi and get down to serious negotiations. This was exactly what the British and French wished to avoid, but they could hardly refuse so eminently sensible a request. Accordingly, on October 9, the first private meeting was held in New York, and by the end of the week agreement had been reached on six principles for the future running of the Canal.

These were : free and open transit, respect for Egypt's
sovereignty, the 'insulation' of the Canal operations from
'the politics of any country', dues to be fixed by agreement between Egypt and the users, a 'fair proportion'
of the dues to be allotted to development, and arbitration
in the event of dispute.

As can be seen, the crucial principle was the third—
'insulation from the politics of any country'. This in-
genious formulation, for which Mr Hammarskjöld was
responsible, offered both parties to the dispute a real
opportunity to come to an agreement and, at the same
time, save their respective faces. It all depended on how
the principle was interpreted, but the way was now
clearly open to a compromise which both sides could
claim as a victory. In private conversation, Mr
Hammarskjöld ascertained from the French and the
British what interpretation would be acceptable to them.
He then wrote, again privately, to Mr Fawzi, presenting
the Anglo-French interpretation, and asking him if he
was able to comply with it. Fawzi's reply was eminently
satisfactory; with the exception of one small point,
which further negotiation could speedily have settled, he
accepted the Anglo-French case. In short, the Suez
Canal dispute, as such, had really been solved by the end
of October. The basis of an agreement had been found,
and all that remained was for the three principal parties
to meet and draw up a definite contract. Mr Fawzi
proposed Geneva as a rendezvous, leaving the date open
to the British and French. The offer was not taken up
—the final proof, if proof were needed, that Britain
and France were not interested in a negotiated settlement. The day the Anglo-French ultimatum expired,

the United Nations published the Fawzi-Hammarskjöld correspondence, thus furnishing documentary evidence of Allied hypocrisy.

*   *   *

Meanwhile, France and Britain were concerting their military plans. According to an article in *France-Observateur* on November 1, there was, at least until October 16, a wide divergence of views. By this time, France was completely committed to support Israel. The Israelis had told Pineau that the Egyptian build-up of Czech arms would make preventive military action inevitable some time in the autumn. Egypt had already begun to transfer troops and arms from the Canal Zone to the Sinai Desert, and to establish highly organised commando bases for deep raids into Israeli territory. In principle, it was planned to launch a large-scale Israeli raid, with the limited object of destroying these bases, some time early in November, when America would be plunged in the last stages of the election campaign, and when the Tripartite declaration, in consequence would be inoperative. Pineau encouraged the Israelis in this intention; indeed, he pressed them to go farther, and to destroy the major Egyptian military bases in Sinai and in the Gaza strip. In the event of such a raid—which would amount, in practice, to a preventive war—he gave assurances that France would be prepared to veto any Security Council resolution condemning Israel. At the same time, France increased her shipments of Mystère fighters from fifteen to sixty a month—thus breaking the arms limitation section of the Tripartite agreement, and, incidentally, her offshore purchase agreement with America—and offered to send in French instructors to speed up the training of Israeli pilots, and to begin joint staff talks. On about October 10, a secret military agreement was drawn up in Paris between M. Abel Thomas, on behalf of the French Government, and a Mr Perès, on behalf of Israel.

But what of Britain? We were still pursuing our attempt—now increasingly forlorn—to secure the leadership of the Arab world. And, accordingly, we were not prepared to encourage an Israeli preventive war, even if this succeeded—as the French believed it would—in overthrowing Nasser. Eden believed that it was still possible to inflict a severe diplomatic defeat on Nasser by securing Jordan's adherence to the Baghdad Pact, and thus setting in reverse the fatal chain of events which flowed from General Templer's visit. And in any case, the internal situation in Jordan was causing increasing alarm in London and Iraq. It had always been an artificial kingdom, and now it was beginning to disintegrate. Under the Glubb régime, the Hashemite monarchy, backed by the Arab Legion, and representing the Bedouin Arabs of Transjordan, had controlled the kingdom. The Palestine Arabs of western Jordan— fiercely anti-British and passionately anti-Israel—made up half the total population; in the past they had certainly been under-represented in the Jordan parliament, which returned a faithful pro-Hashemite majority. But now, with the Arab Legion in the hands of the Free Officers Group, pro-Nasser, anti-British, and representative of the Palestinian West, it was feared that a pro-Nasser majority would be returned at the elections on October 21. What was to be done? If the Bedouin majority in the Parliament was destroyed, a fresh Government would have to be formed, which, inevitably, would call for abrogation of the Anglo-

Jordanian treaty. This, among other things, allowed us to station planes and troops at three points in Jordan. One of the points was at Aqaba, where the Jordan, Israeli and Egyptian frontiers met. If we were deprived of this base, any operation in the Red Sea area would become vastly more difficult.

This was not the only danger. The Jordan kingdom, in its present unstable condition, was coveted by three more powerful neighbours : Syria, anxious to swing it into line with the Cairo-Damascus axis; Iraq, anxious to bring it into the Baghdad Pact; and Israel, which wanted to occupy western Jordan, thereby eliminating the most dangerous salient in her frontier defences and, at the same time, obtaining full access to the Jordan River itself. If any one of these Powers acted, the other two would be forced to intervene also, and Jordan would become a battle-ground.

This was the situation towards the end of September. British policy was clear : to obtain the entry into Jordan of Iraqi forces, which could control the elections, consolidate the shaken Hashemite monarchy, and create a background of force against which Jordan's adhesion to the Baghdad Pact could be secured. The blow to Nasser's prestige might be serious enough, it was calculated, to overthrow him; but in any case it could be represented as a major British victory and a triumph for the Government. After it, a negotiated settlement on Suez would become a practicable proposition.

Unfortunately, the scheme required French approval, because unless the French backed up Britain, their ally, Israel, would not tolerate an Iraqi occupation of Jordan. And if the Israelis announced that they would treat the entry of Iraqi troops as an act of war, then the Jordan

Government would refuse to go ahead with the plan.

This was the situation on September 26, when Sir Anthony Eden and Mr Selwyn Lloyd flew to Paris for private talks. *France-Observateur* later published an account of what went on during these talks. Britain, it seems, failed to secure French agreement to the plan. Mollet pointed out that France had nothing to gain by furthering British interests in Jordan; Israel, even if she agreed to submit to French pressure, would never forgive them, and would certainly refuse, in future, to co-operate against Nasser; in any case, he added, it was very doubtful whether such a marginal diplomatic defeat would secure the overthrowing of the Nasser régime, which, after all, was the prime object of French policy.

But equally so, the British ministers refused to agree to the French plan, on the grounds that it might force Iraq to leave the Baghdad Pact. The discussion was long and heated, but neither side was prepared to compromise. After six hours, it became apparent that no agreement could be reached. But this dismal fact had, if possible, to be concealed. In the increasing diplomatic isolation of both countries, the *entente cordiale* had assumed enormous importance; nothing could be allowed to damage it. It was necessary, therefore, to conclude the talks by publishing a resounding communiqué, which stressed total Anglo-French agreement, and which included some positive evidence of it. But what? There was nothing in particular that they could agree about. Then M. Pineau, with a shrewdness which does him credit, remembered the plans for a Common Market of European producers. From time to time since the war, the French had put this plan to the British; and from time to time the British had rejected it. It was now once more in the air; but, since weighty Treasury advice was against it, and since it was likely to be highly unpopular among a large section of the Tory Party (to say nothing of the Beaverbrook Press), no firm British decision had been taken, as yet. Eden now unwillingly accepted Pineau's suggestion, with the proviso that Britain would subsequently be allowed to decide to what extent she wanted to play an active part in the Common Market. The details were to be left vague. Eden's only other condition was that the communiqué should contain a hint that France might join the Baghdad Pact, a step which hitherto she had resolutely refused to take. The communiqué was, accordingly, drawn up and published; and heavy hints were dropped to diplomatic correspondents in Paris. The meeting was, therefore, hailed as a triumph (though what the triumph was about nobody was quite sure). *The Times* dutifully headlined: *Anglo-French Unity Strengthened. Sir A. Eden's Successful Visit to Paris.*

Eden's mood, on his return to London, was lugubrious. He had not only failed to secure French participation in the Jordan plot; he had also saddled himself with the Common Market, an institution which he barely understood, which he believed would not work, and which he was certain would cause trouble in his party. And the annual Tory conference, where a lot of awkward questions would be asked about Suez, let alone the Common Market, was drawing near.

He decided, therefore, to go it alone in Jordan. And, on October 10, the Israelis provided him with a pretext. A powerful Israeli raid, in reply to a series of recent border incidents, seemed to imply than Ben-Gurion had now decided the time was ripe to begin the annexation of western Jordan. Eden acted immediately. Nuri Said, in Baghdad, was encouraged to offer King Hussein to move in Iraqi troops. He did so, and Hussein accepted. Iraqi columns began to move towards the Jordan border. The French protested, vehemently and publicly; and on October 14 the Israeli Government issued an ultimatum : if Iraqi troops crossed the Jordan frontier, Israel would consider this an act of war. Hussein instantly began to prevaricate. Iraqi troops, he said, could enter only if they were subjected to Jordan command, and agreed to remain east of the Jordan—conditions he knew were unacceptable to Nuri. The whole sordid little plot had to be abandoned. Another—and very public—diplomatic defeat for Britain.

Worse and worse. The Government was now desperate. On Friday, agreement on the Six Principles had been reached in New York, and a negotiated settlement on Suez was looming dangerously near. Public demand for the release of the reservists was growing; 40,000 troops were sitting idle and increasingly mutinous, in Cyprus and Malta. On October 14, the Security Council had finally disposed of the Suez problem by passing the Anglo-French motion by nine votes to two; Russia, as expected, had used her veto. Eden now had to take a basic decision—and take it quickly. Was he going to negotiate over Suez, or was he going to go in fighting? And he could now only go in fighting in the event of an Arab-Israeli war.

A provisional arrangement had been made for further Anglo-French talks on October 17. Eden now telephoned Paris and asked for the meeting to be held a day earlier, on Tuesday the 16th. He flew over to Paris accom-

panied by Selwyn Lloyd and spent five hours with
Mollet and Pineau. The talks were shrouded in the
greatest secrecy. No advisers, interpreters or secretaries
were present. No minutes—so far as is known—were
kept. But, among a limited number of people, it was
guessed that some momentous decision had been taken.
Two days later, Sir Walter Monckton, a known
'waverer', was removed from the Ministry of Defence
and replaced by Mr Anthony Head. According to information later published in America, the very next
morning, both in the Foreign Office and the Quai
d'Orsay, there was a reorganisation of office routine at
the highest level. Senior diplomats found themselves removed from the 'restricted' list for cables dealing with
the Middle East and Paris. Diplomatic exchanges between London and Paris were transferred from the
Foreign Office to the Prime Minister's personal secretariat. A great deal of diplomatic business, it was known,
was now being handled by the Ministry of Defence.
Rome later reported that from October 17 onwards the
volume of governmental cable traffic (in cipher) handled
by the central exchange on its Paris-Tel Aviv link
underwent a sharp increase. Copies of one or more of
these cables, it is believed, were obtained by American
intelligence agents.

The American administration was becoming suspicious. The United States Military Attaché in Tel Aviv
reported that his French and British colleagues were
behaving in a secretive and uncommunicative manner,
and were no longer prepared to discuss with him their
appreciations of Israeli military intentions. Such consultations, which had hitherto taken place at almost daily
intervals, were a vital part of the machinery of the

Tripartite agreement. The President, though absorbed in the final stages of his election campaign, was alerted. American diplomatic missions were instructed to make careful inquiries as to Anglo-French intentions. These inquiries were unsuccessful.

Meanwhile the climax was approaching. On October 21, the Jordanians went to the polls. The Legion was kept in barracks. As expected, the Bedouin majority was defeated, and most of the pro-Nasser parties gained seats. The National Socialists, who had campaigned for the revision, if not the abrogation, of the Anglo-Jordanian Treaty, were the victors of the election, and one of their members was asked to form a new Government. Jordan, it was thought in London, would not jettison the treaty immediately, since it constituted her best guarantee against Israeli attack; but it was clear that British influence in the country was now at an end.

The next day, there was an even worse disaster. A group of Algerian rebel leaders, including Ben Bella, the best-known member of the National Liberation Front, were in Rabat as state guests of the Sultan of Morocco. On October 22, they were due to fly to Tunis for a Tunisian-Morocco-Algerian conference, which was expected to draw up a peace plan for Algeria. The meeting was taking place with Mollet's knowledge—indeed his active encouragement. He felt that the moderating influence of Bourguiba and Mohammed V might succeed in toning down the rebels' demands to the point where they would offer the basis for serious negotiations with France.

Unfortunately, Mollet was not the only one who knew. Max Lejeune, the Secretary of State for War, and Bourgès-Maunoury, the Defence Minister, had been informed of the conference arrangements by military intelligence. On the afternoon of October 22, the plane carrying five of the Algerian leaders to Tunis, which belonged to the Moroccan State Airline, was intercepted by the French Air Force and forced to land at Algiers airport. The five Algerians were promptly handcuffed. This deliberate breach of international air regulations—an act of piracy, in short—was committed, it seems, on the instructions of Max Lejeune. Even Robert Lacoste was not informed until the air-liner was about to land. Mollet himself was not told until the men had already been committed by a military tribunal. He received the news at an official dinner, and his first reaction, according to witnesses, was to exclaim : 'They are mad. The men must be released immediately'. He attempted to effect this the same evening, but there seems to have been an organised delay in carrying out his instructions. The next morning, the bulk of the French Press hailed the capture of the rebels as a French triumph, and Mollet was forced to change his mind. Following a Cabinet meeting the same day, he covered the operation with his authority. As a result, Tunisia and Morocco broke off diplomatic relations with France, and began to give active assistance to the Algerian rebels. The military situation throughout North Africa deteriorated sharply, and the need for a spectacular military *coup* in the Middle East became even more urgent.

Meanwhile, in Israel, the decision to invade Egypt had been taken. On October 17, Ben-Gurion had hinted at the new policy in a long speech in the Knesset. Dealing only perfunctorily with Jordan, which until that day had occupied the centre of attention, he reminded his listeners that Egypt was 'the real enemy' and launched

into a violent attack on the Nasser régime. The date is
important : it was the day after the secret Anglo-French
meeting in Paris. Ben-Gurion, it is safe to assume, had
received the go-ahead from the French the evening before; indeed, it is rumoured that a copy of a cable
announcing this news, and including the phrase 'You
can depend absolutely on the British', fell into the hands
of the American authorities and now forms the principal
documentary item in the State Department's bulky
dossier on 'collusion'.

The Knesset speech was designed to prepare Israeli
opinion for a radical switch in policy. On October 25,
a further step was taken : an Israeli spokesman
announced that Egyptian *fedayeens* operating from the
Gaza strip and Sinai had recommenced their incursions
into Israeli territory. The pretext was now public. The
next day, the Israeli armed forces began to mobilise,
and on October 28, a Sunday, 'partial mobilisation' was
officially announced.

Western reactions were swift. The British representative in Tel Aviv, it was announced, had handed the
Israeli Foreign Minister a note stating that any Israeli
attack on Jordanian territory would automatically invoke the sanction of the Anglo-Jordanian Treaty. The
note made no mention of an attack on Egypt; moreover,
the British representative spent two hours conferring
with the Israeli minister, a fact which struck foreign
diplomats, as such visits normally take ten minutes.
Meanwhile, in Washington, President Eisenhower sent
two solemn appeals to Ben-Gurion to refrain from any
warlike act; it was later said that these appeals led
Ben-Gurion to advance the date of the invasion of Egypt
by six days. Meanwhile a large force, of two-divisional

strength, was concentrated at various points including
Eliat, on the extreme southern tip of the Israeli border;
its movements and strength were observable from the
British military base at Aqaba, just across the Jordan
border, and reports must have been sent to Mr Anthony
Head, the Defence Minister, in London. On October
27, President Eisenhower convened an emergency
meeting of the Tripartite Committee in Washington.
The committee sat in almost continuous session on the
27th and 28th; but the British and French representatives failed to divulge to their American colleagues
information which, it now appears, was in their possession. The diplomatic breakdown at the heart of the
Atlantic Alliance was now complete.

At four-thirty on Monday October 29, Israeli
armoured units, moving in considerable force, and at
great speed, entered Egyptian territory. From Aqaba,
the 10th Hussars watched them go in. The Suez War
had begun.

Chapter Eight

WAR

TO A WORLD shocked and amazed by the events in Hungary, the news of the Israeli invasion came as a surprise. It seemed monstrous and unnecessary that, at the very moment when the Soviet empire was beginning to crumble, the Israelis should have decided to inflict their troubles on the world. But the British Press was quick off the mark, anxiously discussing what action Britain should take. The Anglo-Egyptian Treaty was resurrected. 'There should be no hesitation', demanded the *Daily Express*, 'to invoke the treaty with Egypt, which gives Britain the right in a situation like this to reoccupy the base at Suez.' This was factually incorrect : the treaty specifically excluded an Arab-Israeli conflict from the clause which allowed Britain to reoccupy Suez in the event of war. All the other newspapers seem to have grasped this. It was generally felt, in London, that the Government would refer the dispute to the Security Council, and allow the Israelis to destroy the Egyptian Army.

*　　　*　　　*

The Government was in confusion. The Israeli D-day had been planned for November 7. Following Eisenhower's warning, they had advanced it by a week, and the three ministers apparently involved in the conspiracy—Eden, Lloyd and Head—had been informed of the change of plan before the weekend. The military preparations for 'Operation Musketeer', as it was called, had to be accelerated, both in Cyprus and Malta; and the carefully planned political preparations, that is, the business of breaking the news gradually to the other members of the Cabinet, had to be scrapped entirely. On Tuesday morning, Mollet and Pineau flew over to London to draw up the text of the ultimatum and to fix up the time-table for their declarations to the Assembly. Afterwards, the Cabinet met, and Eden gave them the news. In the discussion that followed— which was long, bitter and personal—those who had hitherto opposed forceful intervention in Suez were confronted with a straight choice : to acquiesce or resign. Mr Butler, and those who thought like him, either had to repudiate their leader publicly—and thus risk destroying not merely the Government, but the Tory Party itself— or they had to endorse the plan with their own authority, and thus accept responsibility for all its incalculable consequences. They took the second course.

By lunch-time, the lobbies of the House of Commons were full of anxious Members, discussing telephone reports from Paris that Britain and France were preparing to invade the Canal Zone that night. At four-fifteen, Eden saw Gaitskell and Griffiths in his room in the House and gave them the gist of his statement which he was to make fifteen minutes later. Meanwhile, some curious ceremonies were being enacted in the Foreign Office. The American Ambassador was summoned before Sir Ivone Kirkpatrick, the Permanent Under-Secretary at the Foreign Office, and told the Government's intentions. He left the room without a word and immediately telephoned Eisenhower. Next, Sir Ivone, with M. Pineau standing close behind him, saw the Egyptian and Israeli ambassadors in turn, and read them the text of an ultimatum : both sides were to withdraw ten miles from the Canal within twelve hours; British and French forces would then occupy Port Said, Ismailia and Suez. If the withdrawal failed to take place, they would intervene in whatever strength was necessary to ensure compliance. 'It was,' as a State Department official later put it, 'the most brutal ultimatum in modern history.'

Meanwhile, Eden was telling the news to the House, against a background of rising booing from the Opposition. There was a reference in his statement to the Security Council, which had begun sitting, in emergency session, at four o'clock, but no mention of the Tripartite declaration. But Eden implied that America and the Commonwealth governments had been consulted at all stages. He explained that world shipping worth £50 million was in the Canal and had to be protected— though he did not say why, in view of the Israeli mobilisation, shipping had not been warned off the Canal. Mr. Gaitskell asked for a recess until eight o'clock to give the House time to discuss the statement; meanwhile he asked the Government to refrain from any action, and in particular to await the verdict of the Security Council. Eden refused to give such assurances. The ultimatum was ticking away.

At eight o'clock, Eden made a further statement, in which he defended himself from the charge of failing to use the Tripartite mechanism on the grounds that he had read in Egyptian newspapers that Egypt did not approve of the declaration. 'Honourable gentlemen', he con-

cluded, 'may, if they like, impugn our judgment. I hope
that they will not impugn our motives.' This was just
what the Opposition proceeded to do. Gaitskell repeated
his request that Britain refrain from taking any action
until the Security Council had finished its deliberations
that evening. The Government again refused, and the
debate concluded in general uproar; the first hint of
the pandemonium which was to fill the Chamber for
the next week.

At New York, in the meantime, Britain and France
were lurching towards a moral disaster which not even
Eden, in his wildest moments, foresaw. Eisenhower, in
a cold rage at what he believed to be deliberate British
deception, instructed Mr Cabot Lodge, the American representative on the Security Council, to block
Anglo-French military action with every means at his
disposal. Lodge introduced a resolution calling on Israel
to withdraw and member States to refrain from giving
Israel assistance. It was passed by seven votes to two
(Britain and France), Australia and Belgium abstaining.
Britain and France then vetoed it. It was the first time
Britain had employed the veto. Next, Russia introduced
a motion calling for a cease-fire and asking Israel to
withdraw behind the 1948 armistice lines. Belgium and
America abstained; the rest—including Australia—voted
against Britain and France, who again were forced to
use the veto. Sir Pierson Dixon, visibly upset by the
proceedings, attempted to speak privately to Cabot
Lodge; Lodge brushed him aside. After the session, M.
Cornut-Gentille, the French delegate, collapsed.

During the night, the news of the disaster in the
Security Council, and the moral isolation of Britain and
France, flashed round the world. Early Press reactions

in almost every country were bitterly critical of the Anglo-French ultimatum. Canada issued a statement making it clear she had not been consulted, and 'regretting' Britain's 'action'. The Prime Ministers of Pakistan, India and Ceylon signed a joint statement condemning Anglo-French 'aggression' in Egypt. It became abundantly obvious, during the night, that Britain and France had sent their ultimatum without any previous consultation with any of their allies.

The British Press, with very few exceptions, attacked the Government. Only two papers (the *Express* and *Sketch*) applauded the ultimatum. The *Mail* and *Telegraph*, normally wholeheartedly Tory, preserved what might be termed a critical suspension of judgment. *The Times* took roughly the same line, and voiced its 'deep disquiet'. The *Manchester Guardian* described the ultimatum as 'an act of folly, without justification in any terms except brief expediency'. The *News Chronicle* and the *Daily Herald* published bitter and categorical condemnations of the Government.

Meanwhile, the country remained mystified as to the Government's intentions. Were we at war? The entire Middle East was covered in an impenetrable security blanket. At three-thirty, Eden rose to make a further statement to the House. It added nothing more to what Members already knew; but persistent and violent questioning from the Opposition forced Eden to admit that no consultations had been held either with America or with Commonwealth governments. Then Gaitskell asked Eden if Britain was at war with Egypt. Eden refused to reply. The House was witnessing a scene unique in British history :

Mr Callaghan: Are British troops engaged in Egypt at this moment? Have they landed, or where are they?

The Prime Minister: As I said yesterday . . .

Hon. Members: Answer!

Mr Speaker: Order. . . .

Mr R. T. Paget: On a point of order. How can we debate a war when the Government will not tell us whether it has started?

The Speaker: The hon. and learned Member must do the best he can with the material at his disposal.

The Prime Minister: I am not in any way prepared to give the House any details. (Hon. Members: Resign!)

Mr Gaitskell: This really is a fantastic situation. . . . The whole House and the whole country are waiting for an answer to this question.

There followed further exchanges, in which Eden appeared to admit that we were at war. Gaitskell then rose, and after saying that the Opposition was driven to the conclusion that we were now committed to hostilities, delivered one of the most magisterial rebukes ever recorded in *Hansard*:

'All I can say is that in taking this decision, the Government, in the view of Her Majesty's Opposition, have committed an act of disastrous folly whose tragic consequences we shall regret for years. Yes, all of us will regret it, because it will have done irreparable harm to the prestige and reputation of our country. Sir, this action involves not only the abandonment but a positive assault upon the three principles which have governed British foreign policy for, at any rate, the last ten years—solidarity with the Commonwealth,

the Anglo-American Alliance and adherence to the
Charter of the United Nations. . . . I must now tell
the Government and the country that we cannot support the action they have taken and that we shall feel
bound to oppose it by every constitutional means at
our disposal.'

The Labour Party was now committed not only to
opposing the war in the House, but to waging a nation-
wide campaign to force the Government's hand. That
afternoon, Transport House set up an emergency staff
to organise mass meetings throughout the country. The
theme of the campaign was to be 'Law Not War'.

Meanwhile, the security black-out continued. The
Israelis claimed sweeping victories in Sinai; but there
was no news of the Anglo-French invasion force. But
in New York defeat followed defeat. On the night of
October 31 (Wednesday), Jugoslavia proposed a resolution calling for a special emergency session of the U.N.
General Assembly. Seven nations voted against Britain
and France, with Australia and Belgium abstaining.
Since this was a procedural resolution, the Anglo-French
delegates could not use the veto. Questioned in the
House the next day, Eden refused to give a guarantee
that Britain would abide by the decisions of the U.N.
General Assembly. Feeling now ran so high in the
Chamber that it became impossible to carry on the
debate, and the Speaker was forced to suspend the House
for the first time in thirty years. That night, the General
Assembly passed a resolution calling for an immediate
cease-fire by sixty-four votes to five—the largest majority
in its history. Britain refused to accept the resolution.
Indeed, the previous evening, Mr. Head, the Defence

Minister, had informed the House that military operations had been started against Egypt; massive Anglo-French bomber forces were assaulting airfields and other military targets in the Canal Zone. On Friday evening, therefore, Mr Butler, the Leader of the House—whose uneasiness was plainly visible—was confronted with the demand that the House remain in continuous session; eventually he agreed to a special session the next day (Saturday).

On Saturday morning, Eden told the House that Britain had received the text of the General Assembly resolution. But the Government was only prepared to stop military action on condition that (1) the Egyptians and the Israelis agreed to accept a U.N. force to keep the peace; (2) the U.N. agreed to maintain such a force until an Arab-Israeli peace settlement was signed and agreement reached on the Suez Canal dispute; (3) that, until the U.N. force was 'effectively' constituted, both combatants agreed to accept limited detachments of Anglo-French troops to be stationed between them. To impose conditions was tantamount to rejecting the resolution, and Eden was again booed continuously by the entire Opposition.

Meanwhile, the country was in ferment. Eden's action had profoundly shocked vast numbers of people, including a massive section of his own middle-class supporters. All over the country, private individuals formed action committees, held meetings, distributed leaflets and stuck up posters. Angry telegrams flowed into Downing Street. At universities, schools, factories and institutions all over Britain, petitions were drawn up and dispatched to the Prime Minister. On Thursday and Friday, more than

2,000 protest meetings were held up and down the country. Post offices reported that there was a nine-hour delay in delivering telegrams to Downing Street.

During Friday, the Government made various attempts to impose a censorship on the BBC, which was, as usual, reporting world reactions; finally, a Foreign Office official was appointed to 'advise' the Corporation on its handling of news. Other attempts were made to twist mass communications media into instruments of Government propaganda. On Saturday night, Eden made a wireless-television broadcast to the nation in which he made a straightforward presentation of his case. Mr Gaitskell asked to be allowed to reply to the broadcast on the following day. The Government whips informed him that Eden's broadcast was not a party political broadcast but a 'non-controversial ministerial statement', to which he had no right to reply. Gaitskell persisted, and the next morning the Government was forced to give way. The "London Diary" of the *New Statesman* reported that "the Government brought every pressure it could to prevent Gaitskell replying, even at the last moment seeking to persuade the Chairman of the Board of Governors to intervene with the BBC executives on the Government's behalf. . . . One result is that the Premier has now made some normally Conservative-minded officials of the Corporation disgustedly anti-government."

By this time, every serious newspaper in the country had pointed out the folly of Eden's action. 'To attack Egypt against the reasoned urging of the world', wrote the *Economist,* 'and under cover of a smoke-screen of obfuscatory statements, can arouse no confident support in this country. The manner in which this crisis has been handled suggests a strange union of cynicism and hysteria in its leaders.' 'Sir Anthony will face a terrible indictment', wrote the *Spectator*. *The Times* grew gloomier and gloomier. The *Observer,* in one of the most powerful and devastating leaders it had ever published, wrote: 'We had not realised that our Government was capable of such folly and such crookedness. . . . Not since 1783 has Britain made herself so universally disliked . . . the Eden Government has become internationally discredited. . . . Sir Anthony Eden must go.' The *Manchester Guardian* had come to the same conclusion; it urged readers to write or cable their Members, and gave a list of all M.P.s and their constituencies.

On Sunday afternoon, Eden himself was provided with an opportunity to measure the extent of popular feeling against him. At a gigantic meeting in Trafalgar Square, estimated by the *Daily Express* to number 30,000, a team of Labour speakers attacked the Government on the theme of 'Law Not War'. The meeting ended with a tremendous display of oratorical fireworks from Aneurin Bevan, and afterwards most of the crowd, chanting 'Eden Must Go', invaded Whitehall and surged towards Downing Street. It was the biggest and fiercest political demonstration in Britain since the 1930s, and nearly 700 police constables, and a force of sixty mounted police, who repeatedly pushed back the crowd, struggled for four hours to defend No. 10. Inside, Eden and his Cabinet were arguing about the military situation in an atmosphere bordering on complete hysteria. M. Pineau and M. Bourgès-Maunoury were also sheltering somewhere in the house. Some forty civilians and six

policemen were injured in the struggle, and twenty-six
demonstrators were arrested.

*   *   *

Meanwhile, what on earth was going on in Egypt? It
had been expected that Anglo-French paratroops would
land in the Canal Zone immediately on the expiry of
the ultimatum. They failed to do so. Not until Wednesday did the Allied air assault begin; and it continued,
without interruption, until Monday morning. But there
was no British announcement of military landings of
any kind. Meanwhile, on Thursday and again on Friday,
the French Ministry of Defence announced that a
military force was about to land. By Saturday morning
it was quite clear that it had not done so. But again, on
Saturday, the French Defence Ministry put out a statement, alleging landings. What *was* going on?

What was going on was nothing less than a total
breakdown of Anglo-French political and military
planning. The following account is compiled from reports
published by Randolph Churchill in the *Evening
Standard*, Air Chief Marshal Sir Philip Joubert and
others in the *Daily Express*, by the military correspondent of *The Economist*, and by reporters from
Le Monde, *France-Soir* and *Paris-Presse*. Keightley
had been told to draw up a plan for the occupation of the Canal Zone, and he had done so. But
it seems unlikely he had been told in what *political*
circumstances the plan would be applied. He also
had to contend with his second-in-command, Vice-
Admiral Barjot, who was operating throughout (though
probably not to Keightley's knowledge) in conjunction
with the Israeli general staff. When, therefore, on

October 27, Keightley was told to advance his D-day
by seven days, he was, to say the least, surprised. But
he set about his task with true soldierly fortitude.
Imagine his astonishment, then, to find that Admiral
Barjot not only already knew of the advancement of the
invasion date, but had, on instructions from Paris,
detached some of the air units under his command to
Israel, for service with the Israeli forces. From this initial
shock the relationship between the Allied commanders
never fully recovered.

In London, there was even greater confusion and disagreement. There were two ways in which the Canal
Zone could be seized: first, by an indiscriminate air
onslaught, followed immediately by paratroop landings;
second, by a prolonged, precision-bombing offensive,
lasting several days, which would destroy Egyptian
military potential before the Allied landings took place.
The advantage of the first was speed; the advantage of
the second was that it could secure the Canal with the
minimum of casualties, both to us and to the Egyptians.
From Press reports it would seem that the decision as to
which should be used had not been taken before the ultimatum was dispatched. Keightley, in Cyprus, was placed
in the difficult position of a military commander who had
been told to commence operations against a hostile
country within a few hours, but doesn't yet know what
form those operations will take. Meanwhile, his second-
in-command, Barjot, was apparently receiving instructions from Paris to urge upon Keightley that he adopt
the first course. Keightley, naturally, replied that he was
awaiting instructions from London. But in London,
Butler was telling the Cabinet that he could not possibly
acquiesce in the invasion of Egypt unless it was certain

to succeed with the minimum loss of life. Finally, Butler agreed that he would be satisfied if Mr Head, the Defence Minister, flew out to Cyprus and assured himself that the operation would be, so far as possible, clean, short and merciful. Head did so, travelling in a Canberra bomber, which broke down *en route*. His journey, which should have taken fifteen hours, there and back, in fact took forty-eight. In the meantime, the whole operation was in suspense. Eden was being bombarded with questions in London, while Mollet and Pineau were sweating it out in Paris, faced with an increasingly suspicious Assembly, and hovered over by the heavy-jowled Bourgès-Maunoury, who wanted to know what was going on.

Eventually the order to commence the bombing attacks was given; but Butler still refused to agree to landings until he was assured that the Egyptian air force, which he had been told was dangerous, had been totally destroyed. The French, by this time, were becoming frantic, as the pressure of world opinion mounted, and as the precious hours slipped away. Bourgès-Maunoury began to issue communiqués through his ministry hoping to force the hand of the British. By Saturday morning, breaking point had been reached, and Pineau, in desperation, flew over to London to bring his personal powers of persuasion to bear on the British Cabinet. He did not succeed; but something he said over the telephone convinced Bourgès-Maunoury that he had, and another fallacious communiqué was issued by the French Ministry of Defence. He was disillusioned the same night by Pineau, who had flown back to Paris. The next morning they both flew over to London together, and this time they succeeded in swinging round the waverers

in the British Cabinet. In fact, the decision to land
troops the next morning (Monday) had only just been
taken when 10,000 demonstrators arrived in Whitehall;
Pineau and Bourgès-Maunoury, to their extreme annoy-
ance, perhaps alarm, found themselves imprisoned in
Downing Street for nearly four hours by a mob of
Englishmen shouting 'Eden Must Go'. Nevertheless,
they had won their point. Early next morning, some
3,000 French and British paratroopers landed in and
around Port Said.

*   *   *

But already the British Cabinet had received the first
hint of disaster. It was not to be expected that Eden's
sudden metamorphosis from a peace-time into a war-
time Prime Minister could be achieved without cost.
According to the *Mirror,* his advisers told him that if
they were given men and machines in sufficient quantity
they would seize the Canal before the Egyptians had
had time to block it. Of course, they said, the Egyptians
had blockships; but all their positions had been mapped
out by aerial photography, and they could be destroyed
before the Egyptians had had time to manœuvre them
into a position where they could be sunk on the bed of
the Canal. Eden, forgetting Lloyd-George's wise maxim,
believed them. General Keightley, he assured himself,
had served in Egypt for many years; he knew. The fatal
Tory doctrine that experience is more important than
intelligence once more reasserted itself with catastrophic
effect. And by Sunday morning, the dividends were
beginning to roll in. As Mr Watkinson later told the
Commons, it had now to be assumed that at least
four blockships had been sunk in the bed of the Canal.

By the evening, the number had risen to six; and it continued to rise, throughout the next week, with monotonous regularity. By Monday morning, Eden had received the painful news that the Canal was now blocked from Port Said to Suez, and that the obstructions would take months to move.

Nor was this all. Eden had also assumed—on reports, perhaps, from Iraq—that attempts to sabotage our oil pipelines need not be taken seriously. Military precautions, he was doubtless assured, had been taken. Iraq had warned Syria, through which the pipeline of the British-controlled Iraq Petroleum Company passed, that in the event of Anglo-French intervention the Syrians might be permitted to blow up sections of the pipeline, in protest, but that they must not, under any circumstances, touch the three vast pumping stations which lay within Syrian territory. If they did so, Iraq would consider itself in a state of war. The Syrian Government gave assurances that the stations would not be touched, and these assurances were obviously passed on by Iraq to the British. Unfortunately, what the Iraqis, let alone the British, did not fully understand was that the Syrian Government no longer controlled Syria, and even less the Syrian Army. If the Syrian Army was responsible to anyone, it was responsible to Moscow; and immediately Britain started to bomb Egypt Syrian army engineer units surrounded the pumping stations and blew them up. The pipeline itself could be repaired within a few days; but the stations, it was estimated, could not be rebuilt in less than a year, even assuming that the Syrians allowed us to do so.

Eden got this news on Monday, followed shortly afterwards by the text of the Saudi Arabian statement that she was breaking off diplomatic relations with Britain and France, and that no Saudi oil would be sold to these two countries until further notice. With the Canal blocked, the pipeline cut, and Saudi oil banned, Britain was now deprived of two-thirds of her Middle East oil supplies. From that moment on, she was—and still, at the time of writing, is—the economic prisoner of America. And, with Eisenhower in his present sombre mood, America was not likely to prove an accommodating jailer.

*   *   *

By Monday morning, in short, Eden had thrown away the last vestige of British independence, and had sacrificed our national freedom of action, at least for many months to come. What of the home front? The Labour Party was repeating its incessant and violent attacks on the Government, and continually forcing divisions. Ministers were obliged to be in almost permanent attendance on the front bench, and were bombarded with angry questions. Labour leaders, working as a team, but led with immense skill and energy by Gaitskell, were gradually breaking down the very physical basis of the Government. Eden remained locked in what might be described as a hypnotic calm, but his colleagues were showing distinct signs of strain by Monday.

Their followers, too, were shifting uneasily. Fully a quarter of the Tories had been shocked and horrified by the sudden news of the ultimatum. During the weekend, they had held anxious private meetings, under the direction of Walter Elliot and Lionel Heald. But these men were in a fearful dilemma. The Conservative Party is based upon a complex and long-established pyramid of principles, many of which had now been broken by its leaders. But at the topmost pinnacle of the pyramid is the principle of loyalty : don't shoot the colonel in the back—above all when he's leading a charge. In this situation, the paramountcy of the loyalty principle made all the others valueless; and the group of rebels, while making their views known privately, decided not to come into the open for the present.

But their position was becoming daily more difficult. On Saturday, Downing Street published the announcement of the resignation of Mr Anthony Nutting, which had been sent to the Prime Minister the day the ultimatum was delivered. Nutting, as Minister of State at the Foreign Office, had been directly responsible for United Nations and Middle East affairs. Hitherto, the would-be rebels had hesitated to attack Eden openly, because they felt he might have something up his sleeve—a spectacular piece of information which would justify his actions and render their own opposition ridiculous. But when Nutting resigned, their doubts were removed; Eden, it was clear, had already played every card in his hand. Nutting's resignation was followed shortly afterwards by that of Sir Edward Boyle, the young and able Economic Secretary to the Treasury. Boyle had the reputation of being the only member of the Government with a real grasp of economic problems. Moreover, during the past three months, he had been more or less in full control of the Treasury, which his master, Macmillan, had been neglecting for the sake of more exciting game in Suez. Boyle's resignation was interpreted, rightly or wrongly, as a sign that, whatever the outcome in Egypt, the Government would be in the most serious economic difficulties, for which he did not wish to be responsible. The Tory ranks began to crack. It was

all very well to say don't shoot the colonel; but the
Gatling was already jammed, and now two of his best
subalterns had gone over to the enemy.

*   *   *

Throughout Monday, the battle in the House swayed
backwards and forwards. From the outset, the Egyptians
had accepted the General Assembly cease-fire resolution,
'on condition that the other belligerents also accepted'.
On Monday, the news filtered through that Israel also
had accepted a cease-fire—as well she might : the
Egyptian army in Sinai was now destroyed or in flight,
and most of its equipment had been captured. But since
both the original combatants had now agreed to a cease-
fire, what were Britain and France doing? In point of
fact, they were landing paratroops in Port Said; the
operation had begun just after five o'clock that morning.
In other words, they were invading Egypt to separate
combatants who had already stopped fighting! And
there was worse news from New York : Canada had put
forward a resolution in the General Assembly, calling on
the Secretary-General to submit, within forty-eight hours,
plans for a United Nations police force to secure and
supervise the cessation of hostilities in accordance with
the terms of the cease-fire resolution of November 2. It
had been passed by fifty-seven votes to none, with nine-
teen abstentions—including Britain and France. Why
had Britain abstained? Wasn't the absence of a U.N.
force the principal excuse for intervening ourselves? Yet,
at three-thirty, Selwyn Lloyd rose to announce that the
British and French governments had sent a telegram to
the U.N. imposing conditions on acceptance of the U.N.
force.

But worse was to come. Before Lloyd's statement, Mr Collins drew his attention to a leaflet, which, as announced on the BBC nine o'clock news the evening before (but suppressed in later bulletins), had been dropped by Allied aircraft over Egypt. It contained the words: 'We have the might and we shall use it to the limit if you do not give in.' In desperation, Lloyd said he would like to see a copy of the leaflet before making any comment. Mr Bevan then pounced:

Mr Bevan: I listened to the radio last night and heard this language, which will have been heard by all the people of Great Britain. Is it not rather staggering that the Foreign Secretary himself was not aware of the language? Was it with the consent of the Foreign Office, or of the Prime Minister, or was it language used only by the soldiers? . . .

Mr Lloyd: I said I was not aware of the language of the leaflet . . .

Mr Bevan: Why not?

Mr Lloyd: . . . but I will certainly look into the matter.

Mr Bevan: Is this not further evidence of something that has gone remarkably wrong with this administration?

Before Lloyd read out his statement on the U.N., Mr Wedgwood Benn had obtained, from the Foreign Office, the text of a broadcast to Egypt from Cyprus radio at five o'clock that morning. He now read it to the House:

'It means that we are obliged to bomb you wherever you are. Imagine your villages being bombed. Imagine

your wives, children, mothers, fathers and grand-
fathers escaping from their houses and leaving their
property behind. This will happen to you if you hide
behind your women in the villages. . . . If they do not
evacuate, there is no doubt that your villages and
homes will be destroyed. You have committed a sin
. . . that is, you placed your confidence in Abdul
Nasser.'

The real intention of the Anglo-French intervention
—the overthrow of the Nasser Government—was thus
revealed. Wedgwood Benn continued:

'In view of the fact that I received this text from the
Foreign Office this morning, will the Foreign Secretary take responsibility for it and explain whether it
does, in fact, lie behind the policy of Her Majesty's
Government?'

  Mr Lloyd: I have no knowledge of that broadcast.
(Hon. Members: Why not?)

The House was in an uproar, with about sixty members trying to speak at once. Then Mr Bevan rose again:

  Mr Bevan: In view of the question which has just
been asked, may I ask the Government to give their
attention to what appears to be becoming apparent in
almost all quarters of the House, that the war aims of
the Government are being elicited from them day by
day, and that they are being changed day by day? . . .
In my respectful submission we have here not a
military action to separate Egyptian and Israeli
troops; we have a declaration of war against the
Egyptian Government in the most brutal terms. . . .

Will the Government stop lying to the House of Commons?

Lloyd now had his back to the ropes, with Labour Members triumphantly coming in for the kill. But he was saved by the bell—or rather by the Prime Minister, who at this moment entered the House and read the text of a flash-signal just received from headquarters in Cyprus :

'Governor and Military Commander, Port Said, now discussing terms with Brigadier Butler. Cease-fire ordered.'

A general or local cease-fire? Nobody knew. Eden could not enlighten them. But for the Tory Party it was the first news of victory, the glimpse of light at the end of what had been beginning to look like a particularly long and dark tunnel. They rose to their feet, screaming, shouting and waving order papers. The Government seemed to have saved itself by the sheer rapidity of military success.

*   *   *

This jubilation was not shared by Allied war correspondents in Cyprus. Of the events of the last few days, they knew little more than the average member of the House. And what little they did know they were not allowed to transmit to their newspapers. The British military censorship in Cyprus was, in the opinion of one very experienced correspondent, the most severe he had ever encountered, either during the war or within the Iron Curtain. All dispatches were read carefully, and if one word was found objectionable the whole dispatch was destroyed. The military authorities controlled all the means of transmission. Some correspondents, attempting to return to Britain in order to avoid censorship, were searched at Cyprus airport and had their notes and papers burnt. None of them even knew how to refer to the operation. Should they call it a war, or armed intervention, or a police action? The censor, asked for guidance, refused to commit himself.

Eventually, Keightley himself gave an on-the-record Press conference, reading from a prepared statement, copies of which were Roneotyped and ready for distribution to correspondents afterwards. A shorthand record was also kept, as well as a tape recording, which was to be used for a broadcast over Cyprus radio that evening. During the course of the statement, Kcightley used the phrase : 'We are in a state of limited war with Egypt.' Immediately afterwards, he was asked if correspondents were to be allowed to use this phrase in referring to the operation. Keightley replied that he had used no such phrase, and when asked what phrase he *had* used, refused to answer. Afterwards, the Roneotyped records were withdrawn for correction and the tape recording was censored.

This incident helps to explain the antagonism which existed between the military commanders and the war correspondents. The latter were beginning to realise that something was going seriously wrong both with the planning of the operation, its political direction and its actual conduct. They therefore received the news of the cease-fire sceptically. During the course of Monday it became abundantly clear that the cease-fire was merely local; and at dawn the next day it had to be announced that, even in the Port Said area, the Egyptians had refused Allied surrender terms. Fighting, it was admitted, was growing fiercer.

*   *   *

But by this time—Tuesday morning—events in Port Said had been eclipsed by an announcement of far greater importance, which introduced a new and fearful dimension into the crisis. Late on Monday night, the BBC broadcast the text of a statement by Marshal Bulganin. Russia had intervened.

Chapter Nine

THE WORLD CRISIS

ON THE EVENING of Monday November 5, Sir William Hayter, British Ambassador in Moscow, was handed a note for delivery to Sir Anthony Eden by the Soviet Foreign Minister. Its contents were disclosed immediately afterwards at a hastily summoned Press conference. The note read :

> 'The Soviet government considers it necessary to draw your attention to the aggressive war being waged by Britain and France against Egypt, which has the most dangerous consequences for the cause of peace. . . . In what position would Britain have found herself if she herself had been attacked by more powerful States possessing every kind of modern destructive weapon? And there are countries now which need not have sent a navy or air force to the coasts of Britain, but could have used other means, such as rockets. . . . We are fully determined to crush the aggressors and restore peace in the Middle East through the use of force. We hope at this critical moment you will display due prudence and draw the corresponding conclusions from this.'

It was a warning, almost tantamount to an ultimatum, couched in the most brutal language, and threatening bombardment of Britain with long-range guided missiles equipped with atomic warheads. It confirmed Aneurin Bevan's warning, delivered the day before. 'If the Government want to reimpose the law of the jungle', he had said, 'they must remember that Britain and France are not the most powerful animals in it. There are much more dangerous creatures prowling around.'

*   *   *

Yet the Soviet intervention, which transformed the crisis and, for the first time, opened up the fearful prospect of a third world war, came as a shock to Eden. He had not expected it. On the contrary, it seems he had explicitly and repeatedly assured the Cabinet that it would not occur. Why?

To find the reason, we must go back to April, when Marshal Bulganin and Mr Krushchev visited Britain. The previous September, they had inaugurated their new Middle East policy, shipping Iron Curtain arms to Egypt and Syria, and interfering, systematically and irresponsibly, in what had previously been a largely British preserve. It was well known beforehand that the principal subject for discussion during their visit would be the Middle East. However, a month before it, their policy in the area had shown signs of modification. It seems likely that the increased tension on the Israeli border, threatening a renewal of hostilities, had alarmed the Soviet leaders; possibly they felt that, if war should break out, it would be difficult for Soviet Russia to remain on the sidelines. Meanwhile, at home, they had just inaugurated their new policy of de-Stalinisation; it was a dangerous and delicate experiment, and its success

would depend in large measure on their ability to preserve international stability. At all events, ten days before
their arrival in Britain, they published a long statement
on the Middle East, calling for a general arms embargo.
It was their first conciliatory gesture since September,
their first indication that they would be prepared to play
a positive and responsible role in the Middle East.

It was against this background that the talks in
Downing Street took place. Afterwards, Sir Anthony
Eden declared himself satisfied at what transpired during
them, and there is no reason to doubt his word. On the
contrary, though details of the talks were never published, some hints were dropped; and it was widely
believed at the time that Sir Anthony had come to an
arrangement—what might be termed a 'gentleman's
agreement'—with his guests about the Middle East. Sir
Anthony, it was said, had told them that Britain's
dependence on Middle Eastern oil was now so great that
any attempt, whether direct or indirect, to interfere with
these supplies would be regarded by her as a threat to
her most vital national interest, and dealt with accordingly. Krushchev appears to have accepted this position,
and to have assured Sir Anthony that Russia regarded
the Middle East as essentially a Western sphere of
interest, in which Britain had, up to a point at least,
freedom of action. Russia, he said, would not discontinue
her propaganda against British 'imperialism'; but neither
would she prevent Britain from protecting her interests
in the area if these were threatened.

Rightly or wrongly, Eden interpreted this as meaning
that the Russians were prepared to give us *carte blanche*
in dealing with recalcitrant Arab States which threatened our oil interests, or appeared to do so. If Nasser,

for instance, provoked Britain, she could deal with him without fearing Russian intervention. This is how he interpreted the talks, and this is doubtless what he told his Cabinet. At all stages of the Suez crisis he reassured ministers, who raised the point, that Russia would not interfere—except in a propaganda sense—whatever we did.

Was Eden foolish to believe Krushchev's word? It is difficult to say. Possibly Krushchev meant what he said —in April. But by the end of October, he was in a very different position; he and his colleagues in the Kremlin faced a real and growing threat to their entire system, and their outlook on international affairs had, in consequence, undergone a radical change.

The fact is, by October, the careful phasing and planning of the de-Stalinisation process had been swept away and dashed to pieces. The process had begun in Russia, shortly after the death of Stalin. It had been introduced gradually, silently and successfully. By the time the 20th Congress of the Soviet Communist Party met in January 1956, the Russian leaders were sufficiently confident to give the process a public and theoretical formulation. The Congress, therefore, was an invitation to the satellites to inaugurate a similar process of change in their own régimes. Centralised secret police control and centralised doctrinal control (through the Cominform) were removed. But deprived of these essential elements in its structure, the Stalinist empire soon revealed its inherent weaknesses: the continued existence of strong Social Democrat elements, who rejected Communism outright, and, above all, passionate and irreconcilable hostility towards Russia.

The Soviet leaders compounded these difficulties by

adopting faulty tactics. They believed it was possible—
as, indeed, it had proved in their own experience—to
introduce the new methods in the satellites whilst retain-
ing the leaders who had become identified with the old;
to effect a change of principle but not of personnel. They
were wrong. Tito warned them of their error when he
visited Moscow in March. He continued to warn them
at intervals throughout the summer; indeed, his last and
most pressing warning was at the Yalta conference in
October, when the avalanche was already upon them.

His warnings were ignored. In consequence, from June
onwards, the Soviet leaders were forced to spend an
increasing amount of their time propping up their
puppets, in various corners of Eastern Europe and the
Balkans, against the ever-rising tide of revolution. The
struggle centred on two countries where the food shortage was particularly acute, and where the people had
daily and ocular evidence of the failure of the Communist system : Poland and Hungary. Poland was the
first to crack. By July, the ferment had risen to the
point where the Polish leaders could no longer control it,
and were being forced, step by step, to give way to
popular demands. As the summer progressed, the Stalinist
elements—Rokossovsky, the Russian Minister of Defence,
and the so-called Natolin group—were forced more and
more on the defensive. Gomulka, the most able of the
Polish Communist leaders, who had been imprisoned
since 1947, was released and 'rehabilitated'. One of his
henchmen, who had also been released from prison, was
placed in charge of the security police. Gomulka was
given back his party card and, on October 19, re-elected
to the Polish Party Central Committee, under pressure
from the party rank and file. From the first meeting he

attended, he took control. Rokossovsky was removed from his post.

Within a few hours the world was startled to learn that a group of Soviet leaders—Krushchev, Molotov, Zhukov, Koniev and Mikoyan—had descended without warning on the Polish capital, and had stormed into the room where the Central Committee was meeting. But this intervention—a last attempt to reverse the trend of events —failed. Soviet Army forces moved towards Warsaw; but Gomulka told the Soviet leaders bluntly that if they attacked the Polish Army would resist. He assured them that Poland would not leave the Warsaw Pact and that the Polish Communist Party would remain in power. With these slender guarantees, Mr Krushchev and his colleagues had to be content. They retired to Moscow as gracefully as they could, and the Russian units returned to base.

The crisis was over in Poland; but in Hungary it was just beginning. From August onwards, reports had reached the West of student demonstrations in Budapest. These continued to grow in intensity throughout September; and when the news from Poland reached the Hungarian capital they overflowed violently into the streets. In Hungary, as in Poland, the Russians had tried to preserve their faithful puppets. In September, they had been forced to abandon Rakosi, who had fled to the Soviet Union. But his successor, Gero, was also a notorious Stalinist, and an object of bitter hatred among the entire people. On October 23, a vast popular demonstration in Budapest got out of hand, and Gero made a fatal mistake : he called upon Russian units, stationed near the capital, to break up the crowds with force. They did so; and from that moment, fighting started and continued to grow in violence. Hungarian Army units joined the rebels and distributed arms. More Russian units became involved in the street battles, which by October 25 had spread to other large towns in Hungary. Additional Russian divisions—mainly tanks— invaded Hungary from the north and east. In factories, workers' committees were formed, and individual 'revolutionary governments' were constituted in various provincial centres.

On October 26, Gero capitulated and flew to Russia; Imre Nagy, an alleged 'Titoist', was asked to form a Government. But here we come to the crucial difference between Hungary and Poland. The Polish Communist Party was able to ride the popular storm because behind the front rank of party leaders—the 'Stalinists'—was a second rank, who had spent many years in prison, who were uncontaminated, in the public mind, by treason, and who were men of force and ability. In Hungary, by contrast, no such men existed; they had all been killed. Nagy proved inadequate to his task; the revolution flowed over his head. The more Soviet tanks he employed, the more appeals he broadcast for a cease-fire, the more bitter the fighting became. Eventually, by October 29, it became clear that he was now a prisoner of the insurrectionary forces which by this time had occupied western Hungary and formed a provisional Government, dominated by Social Democrats, at Gyor. He began to negotiate with the Russians for the withdrawal of their troops. By October 31, the Russian tanks had begun to retire from Budapest. Nagy formed a new Government, which included Social Democrats, announced Hungarian neutrality and her withdrawal from the Warsaw Pact, and promised free elections.

Cardinal Mindszenty was freed by insurrectionary forces and returned in triumph to Budapest.

Meanwhile, a fierce and prolonged debate was raging in the Kremlin. During the early days of the revolution, several Soviet leaders had flown to Budapest to see for themselves. They were deeply divided. The old 'Stalinist' faction, led by Molotov, Suslov and Kaganovich, wished to reimpose Russian rule by force. Mikoyan and Krushchev, it seems, advocated the withdrawal of Soviet troops; they were willing to settle for Hungarian neutrality, and they had information from London and Washington that the West would not attempt to draw Hungary into the Western *bloc*.

Throughout the weekend of October 28-9, the debate continued. But by Monday it seemed that the liberals were winning; Russian troops began to withdraw the next day, and it was announced from Moscow that a meeting of the Warsaw Pact Powers would be held in the near future. The pact, it was thought here, would be 'revised'. Then, on Monday evening, came the first news of the Anglo-French ultimatum to Egypt; and, on Thursday, reports of Allied bombing.

It was alleged at the time—and bitterly resented by Government supporters—that Anglo-French intervention precipitated the final Russian decision to reoccupy Hungary by force. In the fatal debate in the Kremlin, it was said, the bombing of Egypt tipped the balance in favour of violence. Certainly, if Britain and France had not acted, the damage to world Communism caused by the news of the Hungarian massacre would have been far greater. There is no proof that our example encouraged the Russian leaders to take the course they did. But two weeks afterwards, Krushchev told Western

diplomats at a reception in Moscow that Allied intervention had 'shocked' and 'surprised' him. He may well
have been speaking the truth. One of the strongest
features of the new liberal policy was its revised estima-
tion of the intentions of the capitalist and imperialist
Powers. Apparent Anglo-French recidivism may have
surprised Krushchev and weakened his hand at the
council table. In this sense, it is arguable that our action
undermined the position of the liberal wing in the
Kremlin, and so helped to win the debate for the
Stalinists. Certainly, by Friday, the decision to reoccupy
Hungary had been taken. The tanks were streaming into
the country by Saturday morning; and on Sunday the
assault on Budapest began.

But once it had been decided to reimpose Communism
in Hungary by force, the Soviet leaders were, of neces-
sity, obliged to take some action which would compen-
sate for, or obscure, what they were doing. The decision
to intervene in Egypt was an obvious choice; and the
Russians shrewdly guessed that, in African and Asian
eyes at least, the invasion of Egypt was far more horrify-
ing than the reoccupation of Hungary, and that Russia,
by coming to Egypt's aid, would redeem itself for its
Hungarian crimes. Events proved them right: the so-
called 'double standard of judgment' applied by Nehru
to Hungary and Egypt, hypocritical and dishonest though
it is, undoubtedly reflects the feeling of the overwhelming majority of Asian opinion. (Ironical though it may
seem, the only Asians who have made it clear that they
consider the Hungarian suppression a more serious event
than the invasion of Egypt are the Chinese Communists.)

*   *   *

The Russian intervention transformed the Middle Eastern conflict into a world crisis. By the morning of Tuesday November 6, a third world war had become a serious possibility. American reactions were swift. Eisenhower violently rejected Marshal Bulganin's note suggesting that Russia and America should jointly intervene to stop hostilities, and he made it clear in his reply that rocket bombing of French and British cities would be followed by devastating American retaliation. An even more concrete warning was issued by General Gruenther, NATO Supreme Commander, from Paris. Nobody had yet issued an ultimatum; but everyone was getting dangerously close to it. The Pentagon took emergency measures, and American aircraft carriers began to steam towards Europe. At ten o'clock, the Swiss Federal Council issued an urgent message to all the major Powers, calling for an immediate big-Power conference : 'The shadow of a third world war hovers over mankind', it read. 'Peace can and must be saved.'

*   *   *

Meanwhile, in Downing Street, breaking-point had been reached. It was known by eight o'clock that morning that Allied cease-fire terms in Port Said had been rejected. Egyptian military resistance was stiffening. To advance to Suez, at the southern end of the Canal, might take up to four days. But Egypt and Israel had both accepted the cease-fire. There seemed no possible justification for continuing the fighting. This, at least, was the feeling of an influential body of Tory supporters; and Eden was told, on Tuesday morning, that some thirty of his followers would be forced to vote against the Government unless a cease-fire was ordered in the very near future. They had made clear their position in a letter drafted the night before; but in view of Russia's intervention, they decided not to deliver it. Eden, however, was in no doubt as to their views; indeed, it became known that one member of the group had shown the letter to Labour M.P.s during the course of the previous evening.

This was Eden's first cause for alarm. The second, however, was even more serious. Within the past few days, Eden had scarcely given a thought to Moscow, thought doubtless the British Embassy there had warned him of the ominous mood of the Kremlin and the need to repair the Anglo-American rift. The Bulganin note, therefore, should not have surprised Eden; nevertheless, it appears to have done so. His first move, naturally, was to telephone Washington. But here he received another shock. Mr Hoover, in charge of the State Department while Dulles was undergoing his operation, evidently told Eden that, while America stood by the terms of her reply to the Bulganin note, it should not be assumed that American support would be automatic, in the event of Soviet 'volunteers' arriving in the Middle East. Hoover was undoubtedly speaking with Eisenhower's authority.

Eden was now in a fearful dilemma. It seemed clear that, if the advance along the Canal continued, Soviet 'volunteers' would be flown into Egypt within a very few hours. He had little doubt that if the 'volunteers' went into action against Anglo-French troops America would be obliged to support us. But he could not guarantee this; he could not say to his Cabinet 'We have America behind us'. On the contrary, he had to state that America had explicitly reserved her attitude. He himself was inclined to go ahead; if they stopped in Port Said, the whole operation would have been a disastrous failure. But would the others agree to support him? Salisbury and Macmillan were now no longer reliable. Butler, he knew, was strongly in favour of a cease-fire, and he was probably, by now, in contact with the moderates among the Tories. Apart from Head and Lloyd, who were as deeply involved as himself, Eden could rely on no one else in the Cabinet. Yet the decision to carry on the war would clearly have to be a Cabinet decision, in which the majority rule would apply. Outside the Cabinet, his supporters were deserting him. During the morning he must have heard the ominous news that Sir William Haley, the editor of *The Times*, was having lunch that day with Gaitskell, the Leader of the Opposition. Two junior ministers had already resigned; more were expected to follow if the fighting continued. The ship, everyone knew, was sinking.

Such, no doubt, were the thoughts passing through Eden's mind on the morning of Tuesday November 6. Mr J. P. W. Mallalieu, M.P., Parliamentary Correspondent of the *New Statesman*, has written a remarkable description of the Prime Minister in the last hours before the decision to cease fire was taken :

'The Prime Minister sprawled on the front bench, head thrown back and mouth agape. His eyes, inflamed with sleeplessness, stared into vacancies beyond the roof except when they switched with meaningless intensity to the face of the clock, probed it for a few seconds, then rose again in vacancy. His hands twitched at his horn-rimmed spectacles or mopped themselves in a handkerchief, but were never still. The

face was grey except where black-ringed caverns surrounded the dying embers of his eyes. The whole
personality, if not prostrated, seemed completely
withdrawn . . . the overwhelming burden of taking,
on his own account, decisions which have come near
to breaking the Anglo-American alliance and the
Commonwealth have now made him incapable of
distinguishing between success or failure as it has made
him incapable of distinguishing between truth and
lies.'

Yet Eden could not postpone a decision further. He
either had to go forward or back. There was no third
course. The Cabinet met intermittently throughout the
day. The time-table was confused because it was the
opening day of the new session of Parliament. The
Queen drove down in state for the reading of her speech.
The debate on the speech began at three-thirteen, but the
Prime Minister, for the first time in recent history, was
not there to hear it. Various ministers, Eden included,
debated throughout the afternoon in Downing Street.
Their deliberations were frequently interrupted by
frantic telephone calls from Paris. Mollet and Pineau
were now in a state of hysteria. They believed they were
within a few hours of attaining the prize for which they
had worked and intrigued for months : the overthrow of
Colonel Nasser. Allied troops had broken down Egyptian
resistance in Port Said. Their advance units were prob-
ing cautiously along the fast motor road which runs
beside the Suez Canal. Within a few hours they could
be in Ismailia. No serious resistance, they were told,
need be expected. Operation Musketeer had succeeded !
Yet at this precise moment, when victory seemed certain,

the British Cabinet was hesitating. Everything was to be
thrown away. Nasser would survive. And he would keep
the Canal. Algeria would be lost. Their own Government would inevitably collapse.

Eden may have agreed with their arguments but
was no longer able to enforce them. By the middle of
the afternoon, it was abundantly clear that the British
Cabinet, as a whole, was no longer prepared to continue
the war in defiance of the United Nations and under
the threat of Russian intervention. A vote was taken.
Eden lost. The French—by now abusive—were told that
they must comply with the British decision. Eden set
to work to prepare his statement to the House of
Commons.

He entered the House just after six o'clock and rose,
almost immediately, to make his statement. The Government, he said, had received a communication from the
U.N. Secretary-General, informing them that both
Egypt and Israel had agreed to a cease-fire. In view of
this, and in view of the proposal to set up an international force, Britain had agreed to stop military
operations at midnight. There was a great burst of
cheering from the Labour benches. Many Conservatives,
too, rose to their feet and cheered, waving order papers.
Yesterday they had cheered victory—as they thought.
Today they were cheering defeat. They were lost and
bewildered, but their first instinct was to cheer their
leader; so cheer they did. But among their ranks a
number sat silent, arms ostentatiously folded. The Suez
Group, having for the space of the last week controlled
the Government's actions, now saw its hopes dashed.
There were many bitter and angry men on the Tory

side that evening. Eden had taken the first step towards the destruction of his party.

The Tory Press, too, was in a state of confusion. Should they condemn or applaud? As the day wore on, and it became more and more obvious that Eden would have to surrender, leading articles were written and re-written. A leader-writer on a prominent Tory paper, who had spent most of the day in his editor's office, said of him : 'It was like watching a man in process of decomposition.' The *Daily Express* cut the Gordian Knot by seizing upon an announcement, put out in desperation by the French Ministry of Defence, that Allied troops had captured Ismailia before the cease-fire. It was clearly dubious, and was afterwards denied, but by this time the *Daily Express* was prepared to clutch at any straw. The next morning, it announced, in its largest type : *ISMAILIA OURS*. In fact, Allied patrols, creeping along the banks of the Canal, had reached a point only twenty-five miles south of Port Said when midnight froze the war.

*   *   *

The Labour Party was triumphant. They had stopped the war. A meeting, arranged in the Albert Hall that evening to protest against the invasion of Egypt, was transformed into a victory demonstration. When Mr Gaitskell, fresh from the House of Commons, arrived on the platform, the great audience of 5,000 people rose to their feet, cheering and singing 'For He's A Jolly Good Fellow'. For the first time, Gaitskell found himself undisputed leader of a united party. The old quarrels were forgotten or laid aside. The old animosities had

been submerged in the common determination to fight
for Britain's honour. The old militant spirit of the party
was back. A great victory for democracy had been won.
Gaitskell that night was a happy and fortunate man.

*   *   *

The war was over. The world crisis had passed its
peak. The nuclear bombs had not been unleashed. These
were great mercies, for which the people of Britain
could be thankful. But elsewhere, wherever they sur-
veyed their fortunes on the morrow of the cease-fire, the
prospect was dismal. The wild night of orgy was over,
and now the bills were beginning to come in.

Chapter Ten

THE DÉBÂCLE

A FULL ASSESSMENT of the cost, both economic and political, of the Suez war cannot be made at this early date. As Mr Gaitskell pointed out, we shall be reaping the evil harvest for years to come. All that it is possible to do at the moment is to estimate the probable consequences, and leave the rest to time and history.

From a purely financial point of view, the picture is grave. The cost of the military operations themselves, according to a statement by Mr. Macmillan on November 13, was about £50 million; and this seems likely to prove an underestimate. Loss of production through the cutting of the IPC pipeline, it is calculated, will amount to about £20 million a month; the rise in transport costs through the blocking of the Canal and the consequent rise in world freight rates will be around £40 million a month. The *Economist* estimates that total losses to the British oil companies will be at least £125 million; while the effect on our dollar reserves will be a quarterly drain of about £50 million. *The Times*, in an attempt to measure the short-term financial cost of the country as a whole, has arrived at a figure of between £120-150 million, which is based on the belief that the 'emergency' lasts six months. This is certainly an optimistic assumption. An *Economist* estimate of the length of time it will take to clear the Canal, published on November 17, concluded that a period of nine to twelve months should be expected; full capacity-flow on the IPC pipeline will take a similar length of time to achieve, even assuming that there is no deterioration in the political situation in Syria.

The effect on our dollar balance will, therefore, be serious. Devaluation, at this stage, is no way out. Indeed, in his statement to the House on November 13, the Minister of Supply, Mr. Maudling, made it clear that the Government intended to meet the extra demands by running down our gold and dollar reserves. These are already dangerously low, and if they fall still further the run on sterling which the crisis precipitated may well increase beyond the point at which it can be controlled, and the Government may be forced to devalue, with catastrophic effects on the economy as a whole.

Secondly, the oil shortage has completed the slowing down of British economic expansion which began with the credit squeeze in the autumn of 1955. The loss of between 20 and 40 per cent of our oil imports has forced the Government not merely to ration petrol but to cut supplies, in some cases as much as 50 per cent, to oil-burning industries. Some of these, particularly steel and glass, play a vital part in our export trade. It is impossible, as yet, to calculate the drop in production which industrial rationing will cause; but it will certainly not be less than 2 per cent, a heavy blow coming in a year when British industrial production has remained largely stationary.

Some measure of Britain's economic plight—and of our increased, indeed almost total, dependence on America—is provided by the desperate attempts made

by Mr Macmillan, during the course of the second
week in November, to open negotiations with the U.S.
Treasury. Macmillan's object in doing so was to obtain
American co-operation, and, in particular, American
agreement to postpone British interest payments on
American loans, which were due in December. On
Monday November 13, after making his economic
statement to the Commons, he saw an American
journalist, whom he knew to be a personal friend of Mr
Humphries, the American Secretary of the Treasury.
Macmillan explained to the journalist—whose name, for
obvious reasons, cannot be revealed—that he could not
go personally to Washington to see Humphries, as the
news of his journey would cause a run on sterling which
might make devaluation inevitable. He asked the
journalist, therefore, to act as an intermediary for the
British Government. The next day, the journalist saw
Eden, who repeated Macmillan's request. This incident
could not be published at the time because it would
have damaged national interests. It can be told now,
indeed should be told, because it reveals to what extent
Eden's policy has isolated us from our principal ally
and, at the same time, increased our dependence on her.
Never before in history has the British Government been
placed in so humiliating a position.

*   *   *

Economic losses, however, can be made good. But
there are some assets which are irreplaceable. It is
doubtful if the loss to Britain's honour and prestige can
ever be repaired; nor can the public's confidence in its
leaders be restored, at least for many years. If Eden had
been successful, if Nasser had been overthrown and the

Canal seized in one stroke, all might have gone well for him. His policy would have been judged by results, and the position of those who opposed it would have been precarious indeed. But his policy has manifestly failed. Nasser is in power, stronger, in many ways, than ever before. The Canal is blocked, and its ownership is still in Egyptian hands. There have been no gains, even in the short term; only losses. In such circumstances, the reasons Eden gave for his action have inevitably been subjected to close public scrutiny.

They were, from the start, confused and conflicting. In his initial announcement of the ultimatum, Eden had clearly stated that our main purpose in intervening had been to stop the war. But if this were true, why did we continue to attack the Egyptians for twenty-four hours after both they and the Israelis had stopped fighting? And why did we drop leaflets on Egyptian towns calling on them to overthrow Nasser? Why were similar leaflets not dropped on Israeli towns? Besides, in the same week, Mr Head gave another explanation: referring to the Canal, he said 'that is what all this has been about'. Was this Head's view, or was it the view of the whole Government? Still later, Eden said that our purpose in taking individual action was 'to put teeth into the United Nations', and force its members to create an international force. But in that case, why did we make no attempt to get such a force created until November 1, after we had already been twice condemned by the Security Council? Why, in January 1956, had the Government rejected a specific Labour Party request for the creation of such a force? And why, when the General Assembly finally decided to set up the force did we twice refuse to support it?

Later, after the cease-fire, the Government sought other excuses. On Friday November 9, Mr Thorneycroft, President of the Board of Trade, made a violent and reckless speech in the House in which he advanced the theory that British intervention had unmasked a 'Red plot' in Egypt. The immense stores of Russian arms captured by the Israelis in the Sinai Desert, he said, proved that Russia was planning to take over the whole area. But this new excuse was quickly exploded. If the Israelis discovered the plot, why was Anglo-French intervention necessary? Besides, as *The Times* pointed out, the Government's figures of Czech arms deliveries, which had been released in a deliberately sensational announcement by the Ministry of Defence, were not new; they had been published in *The Times* on October 30, the day the ultimatum was delivered. They had, in fact, been known for some months. As long ago as June the Israeli Embassy in London had circulated estimates of the build-up of Iron Curtain arms in Egypt. By the end of September, the estimate calculated, Egypt would have between 150-200 MIG jet fighters, 70 Ilyushin jet bombers, and 200 Stalin and T-34 tanks. These figures had been published in the *New Statesman* of June 23. They were certainly available to the Government at the time. They were even more alarming than the Ministry of Defence figures of November 11. If the situation was judged serious in November, why was no action taken in June? On a number of occasions since September 1955, the Labour Party had drawn the Government's attention to the quantity of Czech arms shipments to Egypt and had asked for action; on each occasion the Government had refused on the grounds that they had no reason to suppose action was required. The last occasion had been early in August, just before the recess. Had the Government been lying in August, or was it now lying in November?

A week after the Thorneycroft statement, Selwyn Lloyd was forced to admit to the House of Commons that the information disclosed in the Ministry of Defence Press release had, in fact, been in the Government's possession on October 29, before the Israeli invasion. This admission effectively marked the abandonment of the 'Red scare' story, though it continues to be echoed, with more or less conviction, in some sections of the Tory Press and in Tory speeches in the constituencies.

*   *   *

The Government's reasons for taking the action they did are, therefore, not only contradictory but manifestly dishonest. Such conduct cannot but undermine confidence in British public men both here and abroad. But is this all? Unfortunately no. There remains the question of collusion.

As has been shown in Chapter 7, the chronological outline of events between September 14 and October 30 suggests strongly that at the secret Paris meeting on October 16 Eden and Lloyd agreed with Pineau and Mollet that in the event of an Israeli invasion of Egypt 'Operation Musketeer' could start. On the basis of this agreement, the French arranged with the Israelis that the attack should be launched on November 7; but, as explained above, the Eisenhower announcement forced the Israelis to advance the invasion date. To what extent was the British Government a party to these negotiations? There seems little doubt that Franco-Israeli cable and wireless exchanges, which are now in the possession of the American Government, indicate that Eden and Lloyd knew the principal outlines of the conspiracy. This information was released, in part, by Mr Dulles in a briefing to American diplomatic correspondents in Washington on the night of October 30; and further information has since been divulged to the *New York Times* by the State Department.

It is certain, too, that Mr Head was also involved. Military intelligence in Aqaba reported the Israeli intention to invade Egypt a week before October 30; and reports, it seems certain, were presented by our military attaché in Tel Aviv. Mr Head's failure to pass on this information to the American members of the Tripartite staff in Washington—or, indeed, to some of his own Cabinet colleagues—seems to put it beyond any reasonable doubt that he, like his opposite number in France, M. Bourgès-Maunoury, was a party to the conspiracy; indeed, it seems likely that Britain, as well as France, gave Israel an undertaking that they would deliberately delay the functioning of the Tripartite mechanism.

There is little doubt, then, that three members of the British Cabinet knew of Israel's intentions and encouraged them. Did their complicity go farther than that? It is now established that France gave active military assistance to the Israelis in the Sinai campaign. According to correspondents of the *New Statesman,* the *Manchester Guardian,* Reuters and Associated Press—to name only four—French-manned Mystère fighter-bombers both assisted the Israeli ground forces in Sinai and provided a protective air cover over Tel Aviv and other Israeli cities. Interviews with these French pilots have revealed that they arrived in Israel a week before October 30, the day of the attack. The French Ministry of Defence, after issuing a categorical denial of these reports, was later forced to publish an amended version, which admitted that French Air Force technicians and instructors had been in Israel before and during the Sinai offensive. On Tuesday November 20, M. Laforest, the French Secretary of State for Air, told a meeting in Lyons that French pilots returning from the front had performed exploits 'of which the public will never know'. An official spokesman later tried to cover this unfortunate gaffe by claiming that the minister was referring to the military censorship. But in that case, why did Laforest use the future tense?

Even the British Government has made no attempt to deny such reports. While insisting that Britain gave no military assistance to the Israelis, its spokesmen have been at pains to avoid any reference to the French role. Mr Selwyn Lloyd, on October 31, denied that Britain had 'incited' Israel to attack Egypt; but he has been careful not to commit himself on the part played by France. Other Government spokesmen, such as Mr Butler, have been content to repeat denials issued by Eden and Lloyd; they appear unwilling to commit themselves personally to statements which future events and disclosures may prove untrue. Mr Butler did not deny allegations about the October 16 meeting; he simply stated, in reply to questions in the House, that the Government did not intend to disclose confidential exchanges between heads of governments. As the weeks go by, as the evidence mounts, and as the denials grow less and less convincing, the majority of British opinion is coming to accept collusion as a fact, as the majority of world opinion has accepted it right from the start.

*   *   *

Meanwhile, the cup of humiliation had to be drained to its last bitter dregs. The British Cabinet had been forced to order the cease-fire, and to abandon its plans to occupy the whole Canal Zone, because America would not guarantee to come to our aid if Soviet 'volunteers' were sent into Egypt. But we still occupied Port Said. When the United Nations voted to create and dispatch an international force to the area, Sir Anthony Eden announced that Anglo-French forces would hand over to the U.N. troops only on condition they were satisfied that the international force was 'effective'. It was assumed in the Tory Party that we would not withdraw until the Canal had been unblocked and Egypt had accepted international control of its operations, and until an Arab-Israeli peace treaty had been imposed. Under these conditions, the Government could claim, with some justice, that the operation, despite its tragic consequences, had achieved its objects.

But it proved impossible to secure these terms. We were now America's economic prisoner. Washington made it clear that the anti-trust laws would not be waived —thus permitting the U.S. oil companies to co-ordinate their operations to supply western Europe with oil—and that no dollar aid would be forthcoming, unless and until Britain agreed to accept the United Nations resolution unconditionally and withdraw her troops with all speed. For a time Eden remained obstinate. But on November 19, it seems, he was again overruled by his Cabinet, and the basic decision to bow to America's will was taken. Eden, gently urged on by Mr Butler, confessed he was suffering from overstrain, and left for Jamaica on a three-weeks holiday. This unleashed the gathering volume of criticism against him in the ranks of his own followers. Randolph Churchill, in a letter to the *Manchester Guardian,* wrote that the only parallel to the exposed position of the British troops in Egypt, hanging on to Port Said, was Hitler's refusal to withdraw his army from certain destruction in front of Stalingrad. 'But even Hitler', he concluded, 'did not winter in Jamaica.'

For nearly two weeks, the Cabinet tried desperately to save something from the débâcle, to extract from Washington some minimal concession to offer to their back-benchers. In an attempt to bring pressure to bear, 120 Tory M.P.s were allowed by the government whips to table a motion bitterly critical of America and the U.N. At the United Nations in New York, Selwyn Lloyd made pathetic attempts to lobby some of the smaller nations. To no avail. On November 24, the General Assembly again passed, by a massive majority, a resolution requesting the Anglo-French forces to withdraw 'forthwith'. America again voted against us. Selwyn Lloyd lingered on a few more days, then gave up in despair and returned to London. The moment of truth had arrived.

On Monday December 3, the House of Commons watched the final act in the Suez drama. Selwyn Lloyd, nervous and ill-at-ease, rose to announce the immediate withdrawal of Allied forces from Egypt. His statement was not so much a statement as a desperate attempt to marshal the tattered claims of the British Government that their intervention had, after all, succeeded in its

objects. But there comes a time when no verbal dexterity,
no skilful omission of facts, can conceal the overwhelming truth. The Tory benches sat in stunned and
angry silence; Labour members laughed and jeered.
When Lloyd had finished, Aneurin Bevan rose to
announce that the Opposition welcomed the Government's reluctant decision to obey the United Nations. His
tone was ironic.

> We sympathise [he said] with the right hon. and
> learned gentleman in having to sound the bugle of
> advance to cover his retreat. . . . I am bound to say,
> in conclusion, that having regard to the obvious
> embarrassments of the Government, I feel I would be
> a bully if I proceeded any further.

The scene ended in a series of bitter exchanges, mainly
between the Government and its own supporters. Captain
Waterhouse blamed the failure of the Government's
policy on the Opposition. Lloyd jumped up and said his
policy had succeeded. Mr Julian Amery described the
withdrawal as 'humiliating'. Lloyd again denied it.
Another 'Suez Group' Tory, Sir Ian Horobin, asked:

> Can my right honourable and learned friend assure
> us, now that we have agreed to withdraw our army
> from Egypt with no effective safeguards for our vital
> interests, that the necessary American consent will be
> forthcoming, in due course, to bringing back our
> Prime Minister from Jamaica?

There was a burst of applause from the Opposition;
Lloyd blushed scarlet. Another shout of laughter followed when Mr Denis Healy asked Lloyd to 'consider
the possibility of putting forward the Prime Minister's

name for the Nobel Peace Prize on the grounds that he
has given a conclusive demonstration that aggression
does not pay?'

This was the end. The next day, Mr Macmillan told
the House of the desperate state of the nation's finances.
Petrol rationing had already been imposed. Now its
price was to be massively increased; and there was a
hint of higher income-tax. The vast fall in our gold and
dollar reserves during November—over £100 million—
meant that we would have to go begging to Washington.
The final debate on Suez took place on the Wednesday
and Thursday of the same week; but it added nothing
new. All there was to be said, on both sides, had already
been shouted and screamed to the point of tedium. There
were reports, before the division, of a large-scale revolt
of Tory back-benchers. But in the event, only fifteen
made good their threat. The rest, swallowing their words
and their pride, trooped lamely into the Government
lobby. For the Tory animal, the instinct of self-
preservation is always, in the last resort, the strongest.
And the Tory Party faced an icy winter of discontent;
only by clinging together could the chill winds of popular
anger be tempered. The Suez adventure ended not with
a bang, but a whimper.

*   *   *

A nation dishonoured, a Government arraigned before
the world as aggressors and conspirators, an economy in
jeopardy, a Commonwealth divided, an alliance shat-
tered; these are the bitter fruits of the Suez war. In one
week of senseless folly, priceless national assets, which it
had taken scores of years—indeed, centuries—to
accumulate, were recklessly cast away. In an age when

our military and economic power is relatively declining, the principal source of our influence in international affairs was our claim that the world's moral centre of gravity was in Westminster. It was not an empty claim. To justify it, we could point to our record in two world wars, to a century of British foreign policy in which the maintenance of the balance of power and the rights of individual nations had been our principal concerns. We had upheld the sanctity of international agreements. We had preserved peace when it was in our power to do so. We had gone to war only to combat aggression, when the resources of diplomacy had failed. And we had enjoyed, in consequence, the confidence and respect of all free nations. In 1939, Count Puckner warned the German people :

> 'Great Britain's rulers cannot use her power in an arbitrary manner. They cannot throw it into the scales in support of something which is condemned as un-ethical by the British people and by world public opinion. If, in her dealings with another country, Britain's policy were ever to be on an inferior moral basis, then the world would see the spectacle of Britain's famed diplomacy deprived of its most powerful weapon, and condemned to impotence.'
> (Count Puckner : *Wei stark ist England?*)

This is exactly what we have just witnessed. Branded in the forum of world opinion as a moral outcast, we were forced, in less than a week, to abandon our attempt to subjugate Egypt by armed might. The real weakness of Britain, so long concealed by our ability to marshal international opinion, was disastrously exposed. We may, in time, recover some of the influence we once exercised;

but never again can we play our unique and honourable role as keeper of the world's conscience.

Nor is this all. A deadly blow has been struck at the very foundations of our society. Our modern democratic system, envied and emulated all over the world, is an effective instrument of government not because of its constitutional construction—which is faulty, illogical and archaic—but because there is public confidence in the men who run it. At the heart of our political consciousness is the notion that a British minister of the Crown is an honourable man. If this is destroyed, the system is fatally injured; its life-blood—public confidence —drains away. In the last few weeks, we have had the spectacle of British ministers lying to the House of Commons, to their own party and to the public. They have lied to the United Nations and to their own allies. When exposed, they have compounded these falsehoods by more lies. Against the attack of a mobilised public conscience, they have marshalled all the worst instincts which fester beneath the surface of our civilisation. Aided by a few debased newspapers, they have attempted to stir up hidden depths of race hatred and violence. And in each and all of these actions they have dragged their followers with them, thus associating with their guilt a party with a long and honourable history.

Our system will not easily recover from these blows. Perhaps, indeed, it may never recover. Our political life may have reached a watershed. It it possible that, from now on, we may follow the path of France; a path marked with ministerial lies and corruption, with deceit and evasion in high places, with increasing public cynicism, with ever-failing faith in democratic institutions. Our national power is declining; perhaps our public standards are declining too. All the more reason then, that the whole truth about this infamous affair should be told now, quickly, before the divisions of opinion have hardened, and while some element of objectivity still remains in the mind of the people. An inquiry can be held. The facts can be established. The judgment can be left to the British public. There are still many of us who believe its verdict will be a just and honourable one.

Our leaders are guilty men. So long as they go unpunished, all of us are accessories after the fact.